To Elle
with Best wish
+ Happy New Year
Robert W[...]

Also by Robert Milton Ph.D.

TIPS—The Imaginative Parent Succeeds
Hole in the Soul (fiction)
The Unspoken (fiction)
The True Believers—The Golden Age of Terrorism
The Reach (fiction)
The Flexxible Brain—Bigger Better Brain via Neuro-Nastics

WOMAN AWARE

Could Eliminating Religious Creeds Emancipate Women?

ROBERT MILTON Ph.D.

authorHOUSE®

AuthorHouse™
1663 Liberty Drive
Bloomington, IN 47403
www.authorhouse.com
Phone: 1-800-839-8640

© 2013 Robert Milton Ph.D. All rights reserved.

No part of this book may be reproduced, stored in a retrieval system, or
transmitted by any means without the written permission of the author.

Published by AuthorHouse 10/21/2013

ISBN: 978-1-4918-2451-1 (sc)
ISBN: 978-1-4918-2450-4 (hc)
ISBN: 978-1-4918-2449-8 (e)

Library of Congress Control Number: 2013918041

Any people depicted in stock imagery provided by Thinkstock are models,
and such images are being used for illustrative purposes only.
Certain stock imagery © Thinkstock.

This book is printed on acid-free paper.

Because of the dynamic nature of the Internet, any web addresses or
links contained in this book may have changed since publication and may
no longer be valid. The views expressed in this work are solely those
of the author and do not necessarily reflect the views of the publisher,
and the publisher hereby disclaims any responsibility for them.

TABLE OF CONTENTS

Introduction: Woman Awakes ix
Chapter 1: Women 1
Chapter 2: Men 11
Chapter 3: The Myth of Protection 22
Chapter 4: Flunking History Lessons 32
Chapter 5: Oppression & Acquiescence 43
Chapter 6: The Hebrew Chronicles 54
Chapter 7: Unconscious Influences 65
Chapter 8: The Newly Conscious Woman 74
Chapter 9: Whole is Greater than Sum of Parts 87
Chapter 10: Awake 97
Acknowledgements 105
Notes 107
References and Readings 151
Index 153

To D'Elle

with love and appreciation for the inspiration

INTRODUCTION

Woman Awakes

That there are, and have been for eons, unconscious forces at work creating the now infamous "woman's place" must be the case. I say unconscious because surely no one would consciously choose slave as a life vocation—would she? I say slave because if the recently touted superiority of the female gender is a fact, then why is it also a fact that nearly three quarters of the world's women are today living in virtual slavery? Why do one in three women in the United States tolerate mental and physical abuse at the hands of a male? (1) Long before written history recorded the exploits of *Homo sapiens;* matriarchal cultures were leading the way to successful civilizations. What influenced the shift to male domination? Male physical strength can't be the definitive answer, or can it?

The other day someone asked me, "Whatcha doin' these days?" I tried to be funny and quipped, "Just waitin' to die." This resulted in a halfhearted smile and an embarrassed silence. *Definitely not funny* I thought to myself as I remembered that my questioner had just lost his spouse to cancer. My *not funny* remark has been reverberating in my mind ever since. I thought of all the ways, consciously and unconsciously, we use distraction, or *try-to-be-funny* quips so as not to think about things like death. Maybe I didn't think about "all" but certainly quite a few. Death may seem like an unlikely theme to begin a book about women and religions, yet every major religion links women with sin and sin with death. In the introduction to chapter ten in this book, the topic of death reemerges. There Richard Dawkins suggests that all of us are "going to die and that makes us the lucky ones."

I personally seem most at ease when I busy myself so that I don't seem to have time to consider some things while I am waiting to die. The unconscious forces at work in this arena are staggering. In fact, most of our daily distractions are of the unconscious or below awareness variety. As Sam Harris, [2] the brilliant neuroscientist, has said, the entire issue of free will and conscious personal choice can be boiled down to "You can do what you want, but you cannot choose what you want." There are always prior causes that determine the final outcome. You did not choose your parents, your genes or even to be born. You did not choose the culture into which you were immersed and, to no small degree, educated to think in a certain direction. Some may invent fanciful Santa Claus theories about past lives, or the like, in order to say we are free to choose or to make decisions, but as Harris said, the basic reality is: "A puppet is free as long as they love the attached strings." Again, "There is always a prior cause!" More often than not, they are unconscious. You may think that "you", rather than your brain's neuro-chemical's, decided you needed a third cup of coffee, but "you" would be wrong. Some moments before you are aware of what you will do next, your brain has already determined what you will do. You then become conscious of this free-will decision and then believe you are in process of making it. Becoming aware of the life events that influence our thinking and behavior, especially the unconscious ones is the major subject of this book.

Why, for example, does a color known as "Drunk Tank Pink"[3] appear to have an unconscious calming effect? Why would individuals, after being exposed to images of money, become more self-sufficient and less helpful to others? In the pages that follow we will address the subtle subliminal ways in which the unconscious has also influenced the imperceptible shifts in gender dominance.

Perhaps the multitude of unconscious daily rituals, available to all of us, has evolved to keep us distracted while we wait for the inevitable. Consider for a moment, your own moment-to-moment activities during your first hour after awakening from sound sleep; you will probably discover that many bits of your behavior are repetitive, habitual, relatively meaningless activities while you are waiting to wake up. This reminds me of the celebrated story of the Buddha. When he was asked, "Are you a saint? Are you a god? What are you?" He answered, "I am awake." Perhaps the real challenge for us is to become awake or at least aware that unconscious forces influence our every action and thought

Traditionally, while we wait, we *Homo sapiens* have been educated to look for, what are often called manifestations of celestial gods or goddesses. Actually, they are common correlations to which we attribute magical qualities. While we are in a wait mode, we are prompted by our ingrained belief mechanisms to project outwardly and particularly upwardly, as if someone or something out there is listening and will respond to our human pleadings. Those belief mechanisms, accompanied by complementary actions or rituals, have been repeated for millennia. In fact, the mere recurrence and constant reenactment of this kind of hoping and waiting increases believability in human myth and magic. Why? Because recurring correlations and our beliefs about them actually change brain structures and thus our perception of reality. Consequently we not only survive, but we insist on passing along our mythical survival stories until they become memes. *No matter where we go there we are.*

Recipients of this kind of meme fabric may eventually be wired or compelled to believe in something extra from another invisible dimension. This kind of repeated mind conjuring makes the fantasy of paradise a perceived reality and even finds gods and supernatural critters within rocks and trees. The Neanderthals, and every generation since, have done precisely this in one version or another. Modern scientific evidence does not exclude all that is, simply because interpretations are sourced in our brain tissue and then reified in order to make survival sense within a certain human demographic.

Some years ago I moved to Hawaii and was repeatedly asked if I'd seen the green flash? "The green flash?" I inquired, tongue in cheek, because I really thought this might be similar to snipe hunting at summer camp—a kind of Island initiation—one of those so-called New Age mysteries "cloaked in its own inherent absence of scientific definition." Some Island mythologies attribute the phenomenon to the Menehune. (The little people of Hawaiian legend.) Similar to forest pixies or Irish Leprechauns to whom magical abilities were attributed, these fables have become a part of Hawaiian storybook legend. Good sport that I thought I was, I waited with the questioner, conversed and watched as the sun went down.

"Wait for it, wait for it, wait for it … there!" He almost shouted.

"Where?" I asked incredulously.

"Didn't you see it? It was awesome!"

Once again I thought this was some kind of prankish induction to Kona life—a rite of passage—indeed a "cloaked mystery."

I waited and watched several more evenings without success. Then another friend produced a picture of an actual green flash. At that juncture I began to think it was another Nessie-like lore-story and some very elaborate confirmation data had been put together by photo-shop for the sake of humoring the *Kama'aina* (locals). Or maybe like the Hawaiian word *haole,* there could be multiple interpretations just as metaphysics has done for a multiple of mythical issues.

Then it happened. After several evenings of obsessive surveillance I saw a green flash! I suddenly became awake to a reality that was there all the time. Since there are literally pages of instructive info on the Internet regarding this real phenomenon, I decided to learn what caused it. As the sun begins to set, light hits our earth at a slightly slanted angle, which means it has to pass through an extra thickness of Earth's atmosphere. That thickness lessens the velocity of the sun's photon rays so that light rays begin to bend, sort of like a straight pole appears to bend when it is partly immersed at an angle in a swimming pool. Scientists, and the guys who regularly study this stuff, reveal that the degree of light bending depends on the color or wavelength of the light ray, violet most and red least. This color differential creates a kind of rainbow prism so that as the sun sets it will recede down the ocean horizon one color at a time, red first and violet last. The experts also tell us that reddish orange and yellow variants are absorbed by water vapor and oxygen. The blue and violet hues are mostly dispersed away from their path by wind molecules. Our atmosphere has the least influence on the color green and that is what, in Hawaii, we see as a nano-second green flash just as the sun sinks into blue sea. All I could say was, "wow". Nature, without Menehune or forest fairies, had used every trick in her considerable bag: refraction, absorption, dispersion and more, to produce this astounding split-second visual experience we call the green flash. I realized that science is the poetry of nature and the green flash is pure poetry!

In short order, I became the green flash expert and started asking visitors to Hawaii if they had seen the green flash. The incomprehensible flash of green mystery was made comprehensible to me and to anyone willing to look for real verifiable answers without appealing to metaphysical machinations or childhood mythology. My willingness to wait and explore alternatives without resorting to magical thinking paid off! Additionally, I had a new waiting ritual each evening during which the so-called "inherently shrouded mystery" was seen as not only un-shrouded but completely illuminated. I began to wonder how many other comprehensible bits and pieces go floating by my brain without the slightest acknowledgement from me. How many bits of data are whizzing by right now without my being awake to them? How often do my beliefs keep me unawake and unaware of empirical evidence?

Another question then emerged: **IF** previously so-called mysterious and shrouded information is now readily available to anyone who is awake, and or aware and many of the so-called "unknown mysteries cloaked in their historically inherent absence of scientific support" are now being uncloaked, where is the evidence that making the unconscious conscious is a change for the better? In short, what has modern empirical research done for us? Specifically, what has it done for the plight of over a billion still enslaved women?

IF uncovering and understanding the multitude of evidentiary data exposes the world of myths and mysticism as bogus, does our waiting to be awakened pay off? Many apocalyptic naysayers and pessimistic prognosticators warn that it is already too late for the rewarding recompense. They argue that we passed the hour of rational redemption for our nation, perhaps for our planet, years ago. Myth and magic still appear to be winning the day. They further suggest that when a single word, such as "hope," becomes a national anthem (4) we should give pause. What are we hoping for? Is it worth waiting for?

Many modern authors have asked, "Why do women seem so much better at waiting. Are they better at facing up to bogus mythology than the other gender?" Actually most experts today suggest that women are better at everything. Perhaps the question we should ask is: how did they become so good at everything? Do unconscious influences affect women less or more than men? Have women evolved a more awakened lifestyle than men? If so, why does slavery still exist for over half of the world's women?

It seems true that waiting to be awakened has become a familiar stance on the part of women. A few women may vocally object to waiting but look closely; for them, waiting appears to be a major pastime. From in uterus to hospice care, sperms to worms, wombs to tombs, women are expected by most cultures to patiently wait. And for the most part, they do. Traditionally women have waited to be asked to marry. They wait to get pregnant and then wait the 280 days while gestation proceeds. They wait for husbands to come home and children to grow up. They wait until the needs of others are fulfilled. They wait and then wait some more! Waiting appears to be an accepted expectation, without complaint, on the part of women.

Our society builds whole rooms called WAITING as if waiting can be equated to Dining, Living or Bathing. We have rooms for each of those activities but, seriously, why so many waiting rooms? Could it be that we build such rooms to provide a practice opportunity related to the quip I made earlier? (Waiting to die.) Should we get used to it? Can we really get used to the idea of death or are the paradise myths the *Homo sapiens* natural way to cope? Have women become more accustomed and adept at this kind of waiting than men? Question: While we *Homo sapiens* evolved, did women develop abilities and talents that men have yet to acquire?

At this point in human history, perhaps we are ready to understand that waiting for Godot or looking into the infinite or even tomorrow is not the exclusive territory of psychics, shamans or some guy dressed in a kitschy outfit. Rather, it is an ability that we all experience, nothing mysterious about it. The prefrontal lobes of the human brain, an area we have developed to be able to anticipate the future, are the most recent bits of human anatomy to evolve. Empirical evidence and the Internet trudge right along with us provided we care to awake and look.

The United States has been called a progressive nation primarily because of the emphasis on technology;

conceivably there is another more significant reason. Perhaps it has to do with the willingness of the more evolved awake female, half of our population, to patiently wait for laggard males to wake up and catch up!

A number of popular female thinkers are saying the time of waiting is long past. They are triumphantly declaring we have arrived at a time that has produced a new variety of female. This new consciously awake woman has never before been witnessed, they assert. Yes, she can concede certain vulnerabilities; but rather than call them weaknesses or even problems, this new woman embraces and utilizes them as motivation. As Hanna Rosin (5) suggested, it is not just an accident that *Sex in the City* was a hit, or that the most hip modern heroine of this past decade was an unassuming, pale, waif-like girl, who was frequently sexually and physically abused as a child. Instead of cringing and sniveling into the encircling arms of a support group or using addiction to numb her life, *The Girl with the Dragon Tattoo* spends her adult life ferreting out and bringing her own brand of justice to bad guys.

IF this is a significant transformation in and for today's female gender attitude, where is the evidence outside of fictional novels and movies? Does this art form really reflect the mores of our contemporary society?

In a recent Daily News article, management expert Jay Forte (6) said, "It's a very service-oriented economy [right now], so you need employees to be motivated." Women are more socially conscious and better connectors than the other gender and more astute. Yet they wait to be directed even while being asked to take charge or "lean in". Women wait. Why? What is the unconscious impetus that causes the consciously awake woman to hesitate? Why do women so benignly accept the glass ceilings**[1] and the wage inequities? Most of the answers to the questions asked in this introduction will be found in the pages that follow: WOMAN AWARE.

**[1] Glass ceiling: An acknowledged discriminatory barrier that prevents women and minorities' from rising to positions of power or responsibility

CHAPTER 1

Women

IF the unprecedented rise of women in the United States workforce has made such an impact, particularly in the areas of politics and science, at least it's been the subject of endless discussion (1) in recent years, what is the significance for women worldwide? It seems to most men, that besides Labor Union hand wringing over wage inequality and the assumed displacement of some males, not much.

IF women are so multi-talented and so smart, why is it that they, after centuries of subjugation, are still not moving to more positions of power and corporate leadership? We have recently witnessed women making progress at a snail's pace toward a semblance of equality in the U.S.A. politic. (As of 2013, 78 in congress and 20 in the Senate) Why so unhurried when every other aspect of modern life is punctuated with acceleration and the craving for speed?

"Look closely," say popular magazine pundits, (2) "the new modern females, as a whole, are poised to make this decade a time they shape, not only their own future, but the planet's survival as well." Of course, such sentiments make for positive public relations and possibly some free publicity. But then, **IF** this is true or even a possibility, why haven't they? "What are they waiting for—Armageddon?" Now that would make for a real load of free publicity!

In some developed countries, including the US, certain members of society are prone to voice a times-gone-by platitude such as, "women DO have a place ... women are, and have always been the power behind the throne." By history's opaque candlelight, that assertion should be: "Women have always been the unseen motivator and motivating agent behind ham-fisted, idiotic male sovereigns." Actually, in many modern countries, the power behind the throne assertion is a Gatsbyesque declaration reeking with subtle chauvinistic undertones. It may be true that in past decades women had been willing to go along with the power behind the throne cock-and-bull story. That was the expected role that certain ever-pleasing, calculating women and their inept male partners played.

A closer examination of this imaginary tale reveals that in our modern age, two-thirds of the world, where The Big Three (three major world religions) hold a majority of power, women, even bright superior women, are still shawled shadows without public recognition. Despite the progress women have made in what are classified as male dominated religious cultures, they are not found behind, beside, or even under the male occupied throne. They are still invisible and still fundamentally indentured slaves!

But surely **IF,** what we are beginning to label as the superior female gender, is so perceptive why doesn't the generic *she* see and act on the illusory source of her second-class ranking? Did she, or did the other gender betray her? Although women in America did eventually win the right to vote, they found themselves, in spite of everything, living in a totally male-controlled social order in which women had been well conditioned in the belief that the male creator had made men in His image. Women were now free to vote—for men! Why have we human beings elected to create and maintain this kind of inequity among ourselves? Even more importantly, why has the acknowledged and observably superior gender allowed this kind of discrimination to persist century after century? What are the unconscious forces at play here for the aware woman?

Let's make some further classifications. We can readily create at least three major philosophical primacies to define our current human condition:

Number one: *Homo sapiens* are special they have souls and will have eternal life in some form or other. This idea still dominates the majority of the world's religious populations, even in the progressive United States. Ultimately, in most religious systems, we always return to the anticipation of death. No matter what language or ideology is used, the concept of life after death emerges because such ideas give devotees a sense of ego centered personal future. This is an ancient belief, which has become an attractive part and parcel of the usual hominid childhood instruction. As any child psychologist will tell you, there are many unconscious forces at work during childhood. Even among the so-called literate elite the idea of a second chance at life, déjà vu, reincarnation, etc., are among the most popular literary themes. (3) This theme in one form or another absorbs the religious thinking of about two thirds of the world population.

Number two: <u>*Homo sapiens* make it all up</u>. With impenetrable metaphysics and arcane New Age proclamations, (4) we are often left shaking our heads when presented with metaphysical attempts to describe reality. For example: *"Today mankind must realize that all matter is energy condensed to a low vibration showing that we are all one consciousness—experiencing itself subjectively. Life itself is a dream and we are the imagination of ourselves."* **[2] After hearing such tautological profundities, most are often left in baffled bewilderment. There is a lot of overlapping within this kind of metaphysical **[3] brainchild and the various world philosophies and religions. Neuroscientists have recently made great strides in bringing illumination to these subjective views precisely because scientists do not stop or get stuck in tautologies during their quest. They are not satisfied with some Eastern philosophical

---

**[2] From a personal Email

**[3] Philosophy & religion are metaphysical in scope and are interested in an attempt to clarify the subjective notions by which people understand their world. The scientific method transformed metaphysics into an empirical activity deriving from experiment a compilation of evidence rather than abstract beliefs.

profound-sounding word labyrinth. Einstein once said, "The important thing is not to stop questioning. Curiosity has its own reason for existing".

Number three: <u>*Homo sapiens* are natural</u> parts of <u>evolving</u> nature and as such are naturalists. (5) Childhood is for most; it was for me, a time of fable, fairy tales, and fabulous magic! I was completely satisfied when correlation was called causation and when I was told, "God moves in mysterious ways." I considered that statement a factual answer and not simply a way of dismissing additional inquiry. I was in total awe at every seemingly mysterious, not yet understood, phenomenon. For me it was magic indeed!

Then, it happened. A grown up person usurped my body and my brain. In rapid succession, some beliefs were replaced with some facts. Logic and a lot of questioning came into being, and recently morphed into skepticism. When I read that Einstein also said, "The most incomprehensible thing in this universe is ... it's all comprehensible." That did it. I knew then that bona fide, real, consensually validated answers were available; it was just up to me to search out and discover them rather than relying on childhood mythology or mystifying adult metaphysics.

The traditional societal and religious impressions of my youth gradually dulled in measured manner while facing the empirical facts that university studies of history and science offered. I admit that today I live in a state of almost constant awe and cuiosity, primarily because I have been blessed with a inquiring mind and have an almost insatiable need to turn over stones and look for evidence rather than just take another's subjective perceptual, intuitive guess at what might be revealed. Curiosity remains my aperture to spirituality. Wonder, amazement and awe are relentlessly given to all of us as we skeptically ask questions and find ourselves standing in a state of spiritual awe as one comprehensible answer after another unfolds revealing still more questions.

I still wonder about the relevance of tradition and/or the so-called modern mystical New Age views in a contemporary, evidentiary and fact-filled world. Even as our daily life is illuminated and described by empirical evidence and provable details rather than magic and mythology, there remains an ambiguity in our contemporary society, particularly regarding the female gender. If the female *other* is obviously required for male progress and growth, why does he seemingly need to suppress and dominate her?

A few men in a few cultures, possibly because they possess intact Egos, will acknowledge their dependence on the female gender—*the other.* For example, the woman's multi-tasking intelligence is often denied. Male CEOs of yesterday's major companies often took credit for what their bright, underpaid secretaries accomplished. A small number of men in modern corporations with female executive assistants recognize that within the man/woman relationship one and one no longer equals two but becomes a more significant synergistic number. This miracle of synergism, created only in the presence

Woman Aware

of *the other,* has more often than not, been denied by ecclesiastic authorities.

However, a minute change in a few modern male attitudes does not begin to address the larger issue. The female gender has been, from the beginning of our recorded history, subjected to conscious and unconscious stigmas. According to The Big Three, today's most popular religious theologies, *the other* was an after-thought in the creation story and Eve obtained rib appendage status**[4] as well as the burden of guilt for introducing sin. As a matter of fact, today in democratic India Eve-teasing is a euphemism for the now publicly acknowledged scourge of rape in that country. The stats are not much better in progressive Europe or America. In the Unites States, politicians often speak of the State and God in the same breath, revealing that the precepts of The Big Three are still impacting the leaders of American Body Politic.

On every comparison test between genders the recent scores are equal or higher for females. The one exception is physical strength. In a time when saber tooth tigers roamed the planet seeking human flesh as protein, strength was necessary to clan survival. But listen *brother and sister, the times they are a changin'!*

As a part of writing this book *Woman Aware,* I interviewed several women who have been outstandingly successful in the so-called mans world. A few months

---

**[4] *The Spare Rib* was the sarcastic name chosen for a UK contemporary woman's magazine

ago I interviewed a bus-driver. She was an averaged sized woman who wore a trace of lipstick and upswept hair. I'm not talking little yellow school bus; it was a huge Amtrak transit bus with all the oversized bells and whistles and a unisex toilet. "Ten years" was her answer to my question, "how long?" Before that, another ten years driving commercial trucks. "With all the computers and hydraulics you only need a little confidence and a little finger to drive these behemoths. No testosterone required," she said with a smile and an air of sophisticated exaggeration. As we move into the electronic age with robotics and drones doing all the heavy lifting, the leverage men held in terms of physical strength is no longer an advantage. In fact, in our age of computers, robots and modular workspace, larger size can be a distinct disadvantage.

With the possible exception of specific times in ancient Europe and Egypt, repeated societal and religious themes of human history have been imposture and sham for women. Today, in many male dominated cultures, we may still observe the circus strongman and the sideshow headless-woman. But they are relics of a busted and rusted out carnival past. All over the world, particularly where prolific male religions control, the blissful Mardi Gras charade continues, even as the data churns out ever-increasing evidence of equivalency of the genders. Men continue to ask and perhaps even hope for a different answer. **IF** women are so superior and so capable, why haven't they made their voices heard the world over? **IF** the human being is the apex of evolution, why the recurrent merry-go-round of assumed male superiority on which we all ride at our own peril, always on the hunt for the brass ring? **IF** we are so evolved and so self aware, why do we perpetuate the appalling history of our so-called battle of the sexes? Why the nihilism in our so-called gender wars and in our treatment of each other and our planet? What is our unconscious demand for any kind of war—period?

Why do we Americans endorse the democratic installation of hypocritical tyrants and then view them through rose-tinted lenses? Even as the mystery of why we need to idealize and idolize certain human beings deepens, it is becoming known that it is hazardous to civilization's survival to idealize events, people, genders, cultures, and certain times in history. For example: American's love affair with their Founding Fathers, like so many other mythologized or deified historical figures, were unreal and/or fictional. They were not all they were cracked up to be. They were certainly not Christian fundamentalists! Let us stop cloaking the past in superhuman fantasy. Thomas Jefferson, (7) like many of the U.S.'s most revered heroes, was a political hypocrite who loved power and hated criticism even when it had the ring of truth. Like other historical icons and their ugly truths, the man who wrote or perhaps plagiarized the United States Declaration of Independence, which enshrined the self-evident truth, that all men were created equal, was also a frequent and fervent buyer and seller of human beings. While George Washington freed his slaves, Thomas Jefferson continued his personal enslavement of 175 men and women on his Monticello estate. He also sold them, many times breaking up families, apparently indifferent to the pain he caused. With the arrogance usually reserved for British royalty, he used the profits from his slave trade to buy French wines and art. Sally Hemings, his deceased wife's half sister became Jefferson's slave mistress as a teenager and gave birth to at least six of his then unacknowledged offspring. While Jefferson contended that "blacks were inferior in body and mind" and that they "lacked basic human emotion," he is still credited with the coining of "all men are created equal."

But what is it that keeps the majority of our female gendered species in a second-class position as if she too is still a Hemings slave on a Monticello estate? Why do most women today tend to assume Father Knows Best? Once again the question must be asked: **IF** the unprecedented rise of women in the United States workforce has made such an impact or become the subject of so much endless discussion in recent years, where is the world consequence or what is the international significance? For reasons that may surprise you, we continue to ask the generic *other* for an answer.

CHAPTER 2

Men

Of all the political systems invented to smooth and enhance the male's status, it appears that, next to the God/Monarch/King composition, democratic capitalism has worked about as well as any, up to a point. Other than physical strength, why do men, according to most written popular histories, even in democracies, hold the upper hand in their control of women? In this age of engineered hydraulics, robotics and advancing electronics, a better question might be: Why do men need control? More specifically, why do men need to control the superior gender?

If we look closely at the 21st century, we see that both genders are rapidly gaining access to nearly all of humankind's knowledge. We must admit that while women are smart and well educated, both genders on average still seem to believe that men should control. That's the way it has been and that's the way it should always be. Believe it! But one recent definition suggests that "belief is a mental deficiency belonging to the Stone Age and completely unnecessary in our evidence based modern era." According to some contemporary authorities, denizens of the 21st century should lack belief in anything, period! We live in an age of verifiable empirical evidence. Progressive, thinking people, especially should act accordingly.

The North American financial crash of 1929 was certainly a challenge to the notion of male supremacy. It was a time when the very structure of the United States democratic society began to collapse and the cry "communism is the answer" was seriously considered as the solution. The Great Depression (1) saw the beginning of the end of a male dominated representative democracy and the beginning of gender parity promised in the Communist Manifesto.

As the male-dominated democratic dream faltered, mobs shouted for the start of something radically new! The march toward communism was cut short by an economic injection from the military industrial complex as the United States plunged into World War II. An unexpected side effect occurred when men went to battle and Rosie the riveter (2) came into existence. The war effort revealed for the first time that women could do men's work in the United States of America.

Infusions of boundless amounts of money toward the war effort meant that capitalism had no economic boundary. As the war wound down, the cry for communism faded. Men, in spite of Rosie's effort, once again took control with unquestioned authority. The postwar 50s were a time of male reaction; Father Knows Best once again became the popular theme of United States culture.

Most political leaders in our current democratic country refuse to acknowledge that the present system of capitalism is almost a mirror image of the pre-'29 crash. Our modern version of Democracy has recently exacted a heavy price from our American society by minimizing public discussion related volunteer civic contributions. It has also allowed the amalgamation of religion, economics and politics. This merger has corrupted the American democratic system to its core in the form of rabid special interest groups, unlimited lobbyist bribes, and unbridled information gathering in the name of protecting its citizens from terrorism.

The contemporary scene finds the melding of quixotic bedfellows. Fundamental religionists and political idealists are even now attempting to uphold and promulgate the belief that economic collapse is still eons away, because God bless America is still a political mantra. Those in positions capable of creating change, live in denial. Politicians and behind-the-scenes tax-evading God-fearing billionaires will never voluntarily surrender jurisdiction over the present American political/economic scheme, even as it disintegrates before their eyes. They suppose that American capitalists, including 1,500 billionaires, Wall Street bankers, hedge funders, tax free religious foundations, lobbyists and every other special interest getting rich off the United States' modified democratic market society will successfully continue the charade. You don't have to be a fatalist to recognize that without a total economic transformation, the United States of America is already imploding and fiscally rotting with seventeen and a half trillion dollars of debt. (And we still keep borrowing!) North America's current herd of young sophisticated but idealistic sheep will blindly and bleatingly continue down their self-destructive path with the absolute conviction they are divinely guided by Adam Smith's *The Wealth of Nations*, and the invisible hand of an ever-watchful fundamentalist God.

Those who understand know that our bizarre political/economic system has been and will keep degrading our traditional values. Today, pricing, buying, selling, and trading traditional values as if they were commodities have scammed devoted American citizens. It doesn't take a rocket scientist to realize that with today's form of capitalism, nearly everything and everyone in the American system has a selling out price. Presently we have a wealth building, hot, exciting, male dominated Politico/Market society.

Today, the logic of buying and selling does not apply to our usual definition of commodity. It spills over into concepts that (with one ka-ching) govern the whole of our American way of life. The new free-market politico/capitalism has tapped into our brains like so many memes. It's everywhere: Politico/Markets are allocated to our health, education, public safety, national security, criminal justice, environmental protection, recreation, procreation, and most other social commodities, unheard of 30 years ago. States now advertise for-profit schools that every upwardly mobile cognoscenti parent wants to purchase for their unique child. Elitist citizens can procure elaborate hospital care as well as body parts and organs, out of reach for the average Joe with ordinary health insurance. Convicted criminals are outsourced to private-for-profit-prison-contractors. America now outsources its wars to private contractors. Today there are private police forces with guns, run by private corporations, which are double the number of public police forces. The über profitable pharmaceutical companies aggressively market prescription drugs directly to naive consumers, a practice banned by most progressive nations.

Profit driven corporations promote eye-catching advertisements in our tax subsidized public school corridors and cafeterias. Tax supported public buses, transporting the working masses, are inundated with commercial ads. Blurred borders, within journalism, between the news, advertising and entertainment industries, get fuzzier every day. Medical corporations now market designer eggs and sperm for assisted procreation. In the halls of congress, corporate buying and selling the right to pollute is a common practice. Current campaign finance laws, which promote the buying and selling of elections by U.S. Supreme court edict, barely rates a yawn in most circles. Greed, and the consequences that attend it, has become a fashionable way of life for politicians.**[5]

Male dominated America is ripe for a new kind of revolution. Some men ask why? But the new revolution,

---

**[5] When *greed becomes the way of life for elected officials, they will create a legal system that authorizes it and a moral code that venerates it"* (anonymous)

now in development, has less to do with any of the economic *isms* and more to do with gender *ism*. It is not the Marxism of the 30's or the feminism of the 60's. That's been done. The new revolution includes at its core a kind of new consciousness-raising that suggests now is the time to sweep aside our gender-ized civilization and replace it with an enlightened progressive civilization based on actual gender parity, genuine evenhandedness and Justice for All!

It is well known that women live longer. (3) Among the world's population according to the New England Centenarian Study, of those who are over 100 years old, 85 percent are women. In spite of increasing stress levels, women tend to live 5 to 10 years longer than men. In the United States, for instance, women now live to an average age of 81. This fact alone supports female superiority in the United States (In male-religion dominated Afghanistan women only live an average of 40.2 years).

The recent economic downturn in United States, showed women to be better financial managers and better employees. Albeit controversial, many experts are convinced that our recent crop of conscious women make superior employees and bosses because they are better listeners, mentors, and problem solvers. Men may question the whys and wherefores, but if you research the evidence by a quick search of Google , it will provide the gender facts available to all of us. (Google: female superiority) A sampling follows:

Woman Aware

A. Many studies have provided evidence that women have a higher threshold for pain, which is considered an evolutionary adaptation in order to survive childbirth. The comedienne, Carole Burnett, in explaining the pain of giving birth, suggested it was like taking your bottom lip and pulling it over your head. (Apologies to males who may be asked to perform a similar act with a lower but still stretchy body part.)

B. Women have a metabolic advantage in times of famine; they survive better because they have less muscle and more body fat. Fatty tissue needs fewer calories than muscle. In times of starvation they burn fewer calories and more fat. As we move toward planetary extinction, women draw on a smaller number of natural resources: water, food and even air. Less body mass means women are ecologically greener than men.

C. Generally speaking, women are less aggressive, less violent and are almost never serial killers or sexual sadists. It is also true that women are safer drivers. (Sorry guys!) Men drive faster, ignore traffic rules, take greater chances and are responsible for the majority of fatal accidents. Women have superior scores in all these areas.

D. Unfortunately, men only have one X chromosome and are therefore subject to more chromosome-linked diseases. Diseases usually linked to mutations on the X chromosome nearly always affect only men. Here, it seems that men can justifiably ask, "Why me?" (Note #3)

E. Also worth considering, speaking of fairness, women are more likely to be capable of being multi-orgasmic without rigorous training.

Men in the western world are still way ahead of most men in the desert cultures. In the previous chapter progressive women were asked to rise up and join together to free the oppressed and enslaved women in culturally stagnate countries that insist that women cover their heads and faces with unrevealing shroud and/or wear a loose black dress known by many of the desert religions as the *abaya*. In this chapter, progressive men in the West are challenged to do the same for their counterparts in culturally stagnate countries. When men in Muslim cultures make even the slightest attempt to update their belief dominated society, they are met with recrimination and punishment which can only be said to have been sourced in ignorance or, at the very least, invented by males intimidated by female superior qualities.

Reuter's news agency reported that while the Saudi King Abdullah (4) is attempting some reform, he faces oppositional edicts from powerful desert religion clerics who adamantly oppose even the simplest freedoms for women. These clerics insist that all civil activities remain in the hands of men, and argue that women should not be allowed to participate in the public sector in any way. However, such religious-based rhetoric has not prevented thousands of women from leaving Saudi Arabia obtaining advance degrees, and then returning to work as doctors and professors. "It's about time," said Aziza Youssef, a professor at King Saud University. "Everything is being held back in Saudi Arabia as far as women's rights."

At the same time, a Saudi Arabian court sentenced two Saudi men to prison (and 200 to 300 lashes) for their attempt to help a Christian woman flee the Saudi Kingdom where the Muslim faith was invented. She was granted asylum in Sweden. In these Islamic male dominated societies there has been an insistence on the use of Sharia law, which allows for both corporal and capital punishment and demands death by beheading of anyone abandoning the Muslim faith. Obviously, for most thinking people, any faith needing physical punishment to enforce its religious beliefs is a faith not worth having.

One of the reasons governments have armies in the first place is to doll out punishment for infractions of governmental policies. The question of whether these polices are authentic, or even rational, does not enter the debate. Most of the time, the function of army training is geared to avoid questioning established authority. An Army can function as a single unit precisely because its members, as well as those who support them (tax payers) receive unconscious educations. Historically, only the least educated and the most economically deprived were sent to the killing fields. It was and still is important for trained recruits to unthinkingly obey orders in order for them to not to think and do whatever they are ordered. A classic military education is generally required of all new recruits. (6) Military education, by necessity, is extremely regimented and linear. Propaganda masquerading as information was/is pounded into recruits and public group brains consciously and unconsciously. As Hermann Göering, the second in command of the Nazi regime in World War II, purportedly once said,

"Why, of course the people don't want war ... but, after all, it is the leaders of the country who determine the policy, and it is always a simple matter to drag the people along, whether it is a democracy, or a fascist dictatorship, or a parliament or a communist dictatorship ... voice or no voice, the people can always be brought to the bidding of the leaders. That is easy. All you have to do is to tell them they are being attacked, and denounce the pacifists for lack of patriotism and exposing the country to danger."
-Hermann Göering, Nazi Commander, April 18, 1946.

The result of traditional training for war is a Pavlovian-like animal that hopefully responds without thinking. Molding the public to support an army to take life on command requires the old drill and kill that educational reformers spent the last century rebelling against. Einstein once said: "Heroism on command ... and all the loathsome nonsense that goes by the name of patriotism—how passionately I hate them!" Yet we still build monuments to so-called necessary wars that have been glamorized and to idealized heroes who have been educated to act on command without thought.

Hopefully after ten years of the most costly, non-resolved war in United States history, some American men have finally learned that killing and brute strength are passé. Cave man mentality is finished. War produces death, not heroes. It is time for men everywhere to acknowledge that their singular superior virtue, physical strength, is no longer needed to carry out feats of combative strength or to continue the myth of protection for the weaker sex.

CHAPTER 3

The Myth of Protection

If genders are considered equal by most progressive peoples, why do some still campaign for special laws to protect females while not-so-progressive peoples continue to rape and murder women under the guise of religious law? (1)

Modern feminists, who continue to argue for the special treatment of women, may actually be providing evidence that women are indeed, at least in some ways, the lesser gender. How do modern women justify the creation of such laws, if women are really equal?

Frail and vulnerable groups may need extraordinary protective treatment. No one would deny that weaker people, children and older people, do at times need special protection, and occasionally some men as well as some women are in need of similar special treatment. But no society should always infer that women, just because they are women, are weaker and therefore in continual need of protection. A closer look into predominately patriarchal cultures suggests, that when we hear women need protecting, it actually means, "Women need to be controlled and/or beaten." Within the desert religions it means ownership, which is the definition of slavery. (2)

On one hand, it has been noted that when conventional men say, Women need protection, they are really saying, "Women are lesser beings and need looking after". In most of the desert cultures, the phrase protecting women is an obvious euphemism for controlling and/or abusing women. (3) When this veiled notion is truly understood it also makes imminent sense that traditional religious men would seek out and reprimand women who refuse to be protected. If men in general see women as needing protection, then they may also have the image of women as the lesser, weaker gender.

Yet, most progressive people realize that if men were to truly view and treat women as equals, that in-itself would remove the behavior that women need to be protected from!

Basic to this whole discussion is the fact that every man owes his life to a woman. These mothers must instruct their sons from birth that women need not give up anything that makes them attractive or female. The instruction that their sons can never own or control another person, especially in the likeness of their mother, needs to be a basic understanding. Mothers are in a position to teach their sons that instruction is vastly different from indoctrination.(4) As the world's mothers agree and affirm that the way their daughters or granddaughters have been treated will no longer be tolerated. When parents are united in instructing their male and female children to adopt new behaviors, dramatic change will be seen in the entire world!

Robert Milton Ph.D.

    Men and women in every culture need to respect each other—now. This includes their freedom and the space to grow without the threat of psychological punishment or physiological stoning.(5) Sometimes it is absolutely necessary for the children of a new generation to weave new kinds of communities in order to provide protection for its younger members. This can mean emotional support or at other times it can mean a good self-defense class. But typically any community that needs special protection for women has bigger problems. Any culture that must enforce its beliefs with violence has no beliefs worth enforcing!

    IF, as recent data suggests, women are so hearty, healthy and smart how did more than half of the world's women come to believe and still follow the doctrine of *'purdah'*? That is, the wearing of a *burka,* wraps, veils or whatever, for the alleged purpose of protection. "Because," comes an antiquated male answer, "men view women as sexual objects who need to be covered in order to defend the social order as well as the woman herself." In short, some of these men say, "women need to be protected from us." In contemporary India and the United States multitudes of women are taking self-defense classes including the use of pepper spray, meaning they can protect themselves.

    What The Big Three creation myth scriptures may unconsciously be attempting to convey is that because women, within the pages of their scriptures, were assigned the role of temptress, cunning and conniving arouser of physical desires in men, it is she who offers the dangerous fruit of sin. It is she who represents the ultimate danger. Therefore, especially in these desert religions it is the men who need protection. The Big Three have traditionally declared sexual drives are anathema and are not to be regarded as natural biological drives of both men and women to ensure the propagation of the species; sexual longing, they say, according to their scriptures, is part of her menacing sinful repertoire and should be avoided like Satan himself.

Many women within The Big Three religions have been indoctrinated to believe that in order to feel feminine and at the same time protected from the men in her culture, she must follow archaic religious impositions. Even modern cultures are impregnated with the mythology of the ancient Hebrews. The alleged original sin of Eve is still with us. Women belonging to one or the other desert religions are required to use the shield of a male relative and/or a burka covering. When this custom is positioned as a religious belief it becomes unassailable; when it is enforced by violence, it is a belief not worth having.

To support the burka as a religious doctrine, some have quoted the Muslim Quran, which suggests: *"O Prophet, enjoin your wives and daughters and the women of the Muslims to draw their outer-garments close round them; it is expected that they will be recognized, and thus not molested..." (33:59)*

For other scholars, this becomes a negative commentary about that particular primitive male society, at that particular time, rather than a fixed command for all time. Most scholars understand the custom of purdah covering as pre-dating Mohamed. In fact, they say, it is a carry-over from a now discarded pre-history Hindu tradition when evidently the masses in their archaic cultures were less structured and more iniquitous in behavior, particularly men's behavior toward women. Even with the protracted evolution of men, most would find such extreme protection preposterously excessive.

Progressive intellectuals, both men and women, in some Muslim societies today, claim that the practice of purdah covering not only stifles the rights of women but also perpetuates male chauvinism. They point to modern India where for eons women were literally shut off from the outside world, and as a result were ignorant of the rapidly changing outside reality. Ancient cultural traditions, such as wearing a head or face scarf, certainly helped identify the brainwashed/indoctrinated gender and deprived her of economic independence. Of significantly more importance, such male contrived ideas obliged mothers to turn out chauvinistic boys and compliant girls. In order to carry on with female submission, women were taught what their fathers, husbands, and sons allowed them to be taught. Today critics see women who still follow the practice of purdah perpetuating a culture where significant cultural, economic and political influence is denied to the superior half of their citizens.

Worldwide fashions, as well as the times, are changing. Countless women in India and other progressive countries today are dressing for comfort. In order to meet the demands of the new global economy, (6) women are learning quality English faster than Indian men. A recently developing part of India's female economy is predominantly centered in computer-organized call centers. Women in these workplaces toil mainly unobserved because democratic India is still a chauvinistic country. It seems that gender-bias and color-tone untouchable scars take a long time to heal. Throughout the research interviews for this book, I found that the most common answer to the question "why" was, "it takes time."

The question still remains, **IF** the female gender is cognitively and emotionally superior, with an abundance of creative energy as most recent empirical research suggests, why do women still put up with these and other subjugating practices for themselves and for other females the world over?

Recently the *World's Women's Liberation Movement* has taken another thought provoking step toward the emancipation of women. Progressive contemporary female leaders are now saying they want the freedom to objectify even as they are objectified. These sexually liberated women argue that if feminists are to be equated with emancipation and freedom, then that same freedom must extend to the male gender as well. Why should feminists, they say, attempt to patrol the imagination of male or female? If men are to be censured for monitoring female boobs, beavers or tushes, then to be technically fair, women's imaginations and terminologies must also be censored! Some other modern women propose: If the ramifications of censoring are carried to their ultimate, we will find ourselves back with the mount sermon where we are required not even to think about sex. (i.e. Not to look upon a woman in lust. Matthew 5:28)

IF the battle of the sexes has been fought and won, where is the evidence, especially in the United States? Actually, a dualist battle of the sexes still reigns supreme in progressive America. Dualistic ideology has been and is still being touted as fact. Women are thus and so while men are this and that. Women must be subtly divisive so they can get men lulled into mistakenly believing they have power. While older bitchy women get on with doing whatever they do, men are occupied with serious man issues. Everyone from Descartes to Freud to Hefner has attempted to convince us that gender dualism and divisiveness on the part of females is perfectly normal and can be best observed in the obvious differences between men and women. These alleged differences, more often than not, leave women in a distinctly inferior position. For example, men are reasonable vs. women are emotional, logical mind vs. sexy body, strength vs. helplessness, etc. These dualistic distinctions, contemporary women are now alleging, have outlived any rational usefulness when applied to the female vs. the male genders. Women, they say, are obviously equal to men. In our post-industrial era the advantage men previously derived from their physical strength has vanished. As a matter of fact, our emerging contemporary information and service economy no longer requires brute strength. Some months ago I interviewed a woman who spent most of her professional life as a type of Government Departmental CEO supervising men in several civil service bureaus. Rather than having to prove her governance while attempting to mediate conflicts between male department heads, where only men were in charge, she discovered that by merely being silent, listening and holding, what she called, a positive thought, the men in several positions of leadership would eventually solve their own serious problems by merely clearing the air. She often repeated, "There is no need for testosterone, since today machines, computers and robots do the tough menial jobs, consequently my job, being a good listener, is really very easy." It appears that this woman's patience and skill set is a vast improvement over the generalized impasse we usually observe in American government leadership positions.

Women who now use their superior skills to supervise men, also say they do not need to be covered in blandness or burkas in order to maintain order. Well, **IF** this is true, why don't they use their influence to make it true the world over? Apparently today's new conscious women no longer want to be defined by their wombs, while their minds assume some secondary or non-existent position. As the above female Government CEO interviewee hinted, "Women no longer choose to keep secret that they expel blood once a month and have sex to get pregnant, and if they choose, have abortions." It seems to be a modern trend that workingwomen debunk keeping secrets and the woman's place, now defined as the old-fashioned male promulgated, unrealistic role for women. They argue that the twenty-first century will see a majority of intelligent, strong women running companies as well as countries. Their grand dream will produce great art, great technologies and great companies. Today's aware modern women affirm, as did Clare Booth, "If God had wanted us to think with our wombs He would not have given us such remarkable brains!"

Another of the women I interviewed for this book is a renowned surgeon in the Palm Springs area. Bright, beautiful and articulate, she could have done anything as a life work. She chose medicine. She referred me to some research done while she was in medical school. This study found that the men who had matriculated into the surgery residency could not realistically compete with the dexterity and skill of most of their female classmates. Not only were the women achieving higher cognitive and clinical scores, they were, to the dismay of some of her older conventional male mentors, more competent in dealing with emotional crises in the emergency room.

IF women have such remarkable brains, talent and emotional stability, why is the United States society, particularly the male political leaders reared by these remarkable brained women, so messed up with respect to the treatment of women? The answer comes from studies that define the new emerging woman and her varying role in an ever-shifting economy. (7) Perhaps the new problems we face are male fixation rather than female flexibility.

We all know that individual preferences enter into the scheme of these things, especially when it comes to what turns a woman on sexually. The modern American woman, on one hand, appears to be rising above base animalistic passions. Allegedly this is a philosophy possessed only by insensitive men. On the other hand, the recent blockbusting success of *Fifty Shades of Grey* (8) advocates for an enormous middle ground of women who apparently masturbate but still want men with panty busting smiles and who know what it means to be a natural-born yoni-tapper! The recent *What Women Want* (9) suggests that modern science can prove that women are just as randy as men ever were.

Still, there are uncomfortable, politically incorrect conclusions that spring from those and other recent best selling pages. Today, it is said, when an ascendant career woman arrives home, she now expects a waiting cocktail and a guy who can be multi talented. Some of these new women want to be adored as well as to adore and have sex on their terms and, sometimes, his. She wants to know that in her safe harbor home, security, candlelit baths and open sensuality are part of her daily reality. She wants what men have always claimed as theirs exclusively. Why should desiring this idyllic standard, which women now feel should be theirs, result in criticism? (10) A better question might be: **IF** women are so smart and insightful, why do they desire to repeat a pattern that is exactly what they are objecting to when men do it?

CHAPTER 4

Flunking History Lessons

It is said that women have many unique, natural, intuitive gifts of knowing. It is also said that their alternative ways of knowing are different in name only and ultimately lead to the same universal truths. But, is the intuitive way, for example, or the Hindu Vedic way, simply alternative ways of knowing what Jews, Christians or Muslims (The Big Three) teach? The question we must ask is: Where is the empirical evidence regarding intuition, particularly woman's intuition?

I would like to approach women's unique gifts though an alternative and more outlying access. If women in modern New Age America or ancient Hindu India or any of the worlds more progressive countries are better educated, marry later by choice, and live longer than men, why are they so often treated so poorly in the public and political arena? An article written by Kalpana Sharma for *The Hindu News,* an English-language Indian newspaper founded and continuously published since 1879, alleges that Indian women are groped and pinched by males wherever they go in public. The myth, according to the article, particularly prevalent in modern

India, is that women have slowly gained equivalent status with men. They are now supposed to be treated as equals. Yet, reportedly in India's most progressive state. Kerala, women can't go anywhere alone without being accosted or molested. Even in the region where women have made the greatest strides in employment and education, they allegedly cannot step out of their homes or offices without fear of being assaulted. The record is hardly better in many college campuses in the United States or in many of Europe's more progressive countries. (1)

A more bona fide question might be, is this Hindu religion sponsored Newspaper survey reliable or just more propaganda to keep women afraid of their male dominated Hindu culture? Most in-the-know United States citizens take American newspaper surveys with more than a grain of salt. Various surveys in the United States suggest that about half of its populace believe in a personal god while an even larger percentage believe in spirits, ghosts and other supernatural powers. (2)

About an equal number, according to American surveys, believe that women are substandard when compared to men. More salt please! At the same time, it appears that advanced education is highly correlated with agnosticism rather than faith. (3) As the United States population becomes more educated the surveys related to supernatural phenomena of any sort appear to be diminishing in number.

The word science is once again being used to affirm a literal truth of sacred scriptures and holy books, particularly in the United States and India. The grass roots campaign to teach holy-book creationism in America is well known. Perhaps less well known is that recently Indian Vedic science has become a noticeable trend in English speaking countries such as India, the U.S. and the U.K. New Age and Krishna-type movements are also in evidence; even the best selling author, Deepak Chopra, has defended a form of *intelligent design* from a Hindu perspective. (4)

The trendy belief that astrology, spiritualism, numerology, Vedic medicine and other esoteric ancient teachings have validity and are in complete concert with legitimate modern science and continues to absorb space in popular magazines. In short, there is a popular attempt to create science in the image of a new religion.

With this trend, the notorious and denied caste system in India, which involves all forms of subjugation, especially for women, also grows. Recent renewed belief in God-given sacred scriptures is evidently on the rise these days in India as well as in segments of the United States population. This kind of resurgence of God, religion and faith oriented science raises a hugely discomforting question: Why? Why do we keep repeating this same illogical behavior expecting a different outcome? Is this a new form of insanity? Or, is the not-so-subtle rising of women's status one of the focal point concerns in this rise of faith-oriented science?

Until recently, in India and the United States, science and modernity, rather than magic, were making unassuming progress. It has always been a basic understanding of progressive educators that as humans continued to abandon myth and superstition, the world at large would become more evidence based. As a case in point, most scientists assumed enlightened people in general would no longer blindly believe in magic and supernatural non-sense. Thus as societies became more evidence based and progressive, religion and metaphysics would lose their alleged value. For decades the intellectual giants appeared to be of one opinion: Religion and supernatural magic would have little, if any, value in an educated, progressive, open-minded future. It has been asserted that the future belongs to rational thought.

Recently it has also been noted that the rise of Vedic conversant women is now being correlated with what one Indian science writer called a "backward march to believe rather than reason." (5) This correlation raises some interesting questions: **IF** secularism is basically an attitude of parsimony or minimalism, and **IF** modern women are espousing evidence rather than blind belief along with their independence, why this "backward march?" Since there has never been any empirical evidence for the existence of anthropomorphic gods, shouldn't myths, magic and female subjugation be laid aside as a non-productive history? Modern secularists, including modern progressive women, assumed Occam's razor would apply. **IF** this is true, why have not the labyrinthine-like metaphysical schemes been put aside for more parsimonious explanations and evidence?

Part of the answer can be found in the repeated haranguing of select groups. For example, modern religious fundamentalists, and the American New Agers, keep shouting, your faith is as important as your reasoning. General populations of women in democratically organized countries have begun asking, "Should we women trust what we are told by those who say they have answers e.g. unchanging, fixed religionists, or should we throw our hats in the ring with curious scientists who seem to change their theories at the drop of that same hat? Many devout fans of mysticism are taking liberties with the language of science, particularly quantum physics, to reach uber-belief status. Those scientists who demonstrate that consciousness, the self and the direct intuition of ultimate meaning are sourced in our own brain activity become vulnerable to castigation. Both traditional churchgoers and those of the more fashionable postmodern metaphysical persuasions often refuse neuroscience evidence.

After all, it is said that women are the intuitive gender. These same select groups make use of this designation. In a very real way it's become their new mantra. "Use your intuition!" Which, for many, means don't worry about rationality, especially when emotionality and contemplation fits better with the new tune. (6)

Apparently, progressive secularists mistakenly assumed that as modern women were increasingly esteemed and educated, they would find it implausible to retreat to the idea of second-class citizenry merely because those in-the-know said the supreme male god decreed it. But now, according to Dr. Nanda, some popular liberated women are saying intuition and belief are equally as important as empirical fact and coherent logic. A few fashionable female leaders are even suggesting that the incorporation of progressive thought does not mean the revered and sacred dictums of old religion need to be abandoned. In fact, they say, quoting Einstein, "Imagination is more important than knowledge."

The very bedrock of what constitutes empirical evidence, how and of what it is constructed, and its impact on the ascendance of the female gender is now being re-questioned by select groups the world over. Historically, almost unnoticed by the masses, a slow deterioration of male superiority and female inferiority in scientific spheres was a fact. Equality issues were virtually nonexistent in the context of scientific research institutions worldwide.

However, recently in several local communities, religious leaders are contending that their regional cultural science and ancient healing systems have newly discovered validity. Alongside these claims comes the suggestion that cultural science and belief can once again legitimize patriarchal power. How? As politicians and religious leaders of Indian, Chinese and Muslim satellite countries denounce western science as the devil in disguise, these recently popularized religious views are becoming accepted by multitudes in these populations. Fashionable non-empirically based propaganda encourages the acceptance of alternative ways of *knowing*. This is also becoming trendy with the so-called New Age groups in America. Meera Nanda seemed almost prescient when she alleged, "When ancient mythology, metaphysics and cultish truth systems are dignified by suggesting they have an equivalent parlance with empirical evidence, there is no safety net to catch emerging, modernizing cultures from falling backward and downward into tribalism and sectarianism; which more often than not, subverts the female gender to second-rate citizenship positions." Perceptive Einstein, as if speaking to our modern anti-science sources sardonically said, "If the facts don't fit the theory, change the facts."

As was said above, a number of liberated women are announcing that they can now appreciate mysticism as an alternative way of knowing. Further, some suggest that the incorporation of secularism does not mean their sacred beliefs need fade away. That being said, notwithstanding intuition and New Age contentions, when viewed objectively, the acknowledgment of empirical evidence does mean that faith belief terms lose their supernatural value and control in political decision-making.

For most secularists, so-called sacred concepts and the word spiritual are seen as being similar to Einstein's poetic metaphor for perpetual wonder (i.e. God doesn't play dice). For most progressives, spirituality means to be in a continuous state of curiosity and discovery and, therefore, in a constant state of awe. Reverence for the wonders of life and nature thus provide an interminable cycle to those who truly recognize curiosity and discovery as their personal source of spirituality. More often than not, women are the first to experience and understand this spiritual cycle, through the process of naissance, the birthing of new human life.

Political powers, particularly men around the world, are putting their loss of power at the doorstep of scientific enlightenment. It may come as a surprise to some who are familiar with the importance of natural law and science in the origins of each of the above mentioned cultures, in India, Hindu nationalists are now passionately obsessed with traditional *Vedic science* in the same way fundamental religionists in the West are obsessed with their scriptural Creation science.

Especially in emerging cultures, with a history of male dominate religion, there appears to be a desperate urge to denounce Western science, particularly the concept of evolution-based biology and physics. These deprecating denouncements subtly suppress the feminine movement while proving that their localized, time-honored, cultural sciences are valid, or at the very least, alternative ways of knowing. This new culture-based science inevitably substantiates the metaphysical ramblings of sacred holy book mythology while denouncing empirical science as anti-spiritual.

In India, as well as America, popular vote-seeking politicians unabashedly proclaim Vedic Hinduism and Creationism are simply science by another name. (7) Professed New Age supporters in the U.S. often aid these claims. Rather than take the contradictions between empirical evidence and the cultural traditions at face value, American religionists, now called by many alternative names, deny that there is any contradiction at all. It is just an alternative way of knowing, they say.

Being accepting of this kind of multiplicity results in Vedic science being pushed in colleges, free-thought churches, and mass media. If this form of metaphysical religious thought is defined as science then it is only fair that Muslim and Christian holy book science be accepted as well.

In the opinion of progressives, the definition of empirical science and the continued liberation of the female gender are too important to be left to magic and/or religious fantasy. Yet, how popular is the celebrated religious idea that different ways of knowledge are different only in name and lead to the same universal truth? You've undoubtedly heard this proclamation about different paths leading to the same destination; but does it walk on all fours?

Dr. Meera Nanda's book, *Prophets Facing Backwards,* suggests that the answer to the above question is a resounding No! She is a bona fide Indian science writer and philosopher, an unusual combination for someone who advocates the universality of empirical science as a remedy to the recent resurgence of religion/cultural fragmentation taking place in India and America. She argues that the ever-growing Hindu nationalistic practice of claiming that their Vedic sciences based on Hindu holy books (e.g. astrology, ayurvedic medicine, faith healing and telepathy), are just as valid as modern

Western science is a "backward march." Vedic science, she asserts, is a "phony face on age old superstition".

As suggested earlier, when liberated women and Western intellectuals begin to use political acceptance of diversity to exalt local metaphysical truth systems over the universality of empirical evidence, these emerging societies will begin a backward decline into religious sectarianism.

Even a fleeting look at the plethora of worldwide religious hatreds advises us that an empirical secular way of knowing, that makes no allusion to the gods or in the case of Hinduism's caste system, accidents of birth, is a priceless gift. Nanda asserts this "gift is under assault." Because, she asserts, what looks like Politically Correct tolerance and nonjudgmental, tacit consent to be different is in reality a condescending act on the part of Western religious fundamentalists. Nanda says this kind of political correctness "denies ... the capacity and the need for a reasoned modification of holy-book cosmologies in the light of better evidence, offered by the empirical method." She suggests that any distinct way of knowing that secularizes nature, serves oppressed people everywhere, particularly women. The questioning of tradition, and the acceptance of mounting empirical evidence, is gradually breaking the hold of those, particularly males, whose claim of domination presumes a male God's divine favor. Nanda also says that around the world, ancient male dominated cultures are aggressively attempting to modernize their so-called sacred philosophies and even more aggressively re-traditionalizing their cultural religious institutions. We must now wonder: Is part of the motivation for this Vedic or bible science resurgence to preserve the good-ol'-boy institutions and keep the newly rising *Woman Aware* in her subservient place?

CHAPTER 5

Oppression & Acquiescence

IF, as modern pop-science would have us believe, contemporary women's mental capacities are evolving at a faster rate than men, where is the world-wide, universal evidence? A recent study revealed that women are also getting better looking by today's standards, through evolution; meanwhile, men are staying the same. Dazzling daughters mean more gorgeous women for the next generations. That same study revealed, "Women evolve 'hotter' than their male counterparts." (1) After following more than 2,000 modern hominids through four decades of life, attractive females had 16 percent more children than average-looking females, and furthermore attractive people are 36 percent more probable to have firstborn daughters.

The modern female brain is also said to be evolving in a direction where subservience is an outmoded construct and women themselves are evolving toward something superior. Where is the evidence for the entire female world population, especially among the desert religions? Why is today's empirical evidence for the improved female limited to democratic-progressive societies?

IF it is accepted that "one is not born, but rather becomes a woman" as Simone de Beauvoir alleged in her classic opus *The Second Sex* (2) and that becoming is part and parcel of a modern non-acquiescent life, and **IF** as Sheryl Sandberg proclaims in her new best seller *Lean In*, women are not genetically inferior in the market place but rather become inferior by failing to take their "rightful place at the table." (3) Then again, it must be asked, where is the worldwide evidence?

The United States is considered by many to be one of the world's most progressive countries and is allegedly facilitating the assignment of leadership to women. **IF** this is the reality, why has the second-class status statistic for numbers of women in the U.S. and in most of the developed world remained relatively unchanged for the last three decades? Why has the near-slave status of all women in over half of the world remained entrenched or worsened? Not only do American females have little or no influence in Muslim countries, it appears the influence is going in a negative direction as citizens in progressive countries are taught that it is politically correct (PC) to be accepting of Islamic religious demands. Basically, women are required to be compliant to men's demands because, according to their religious dictates, they are the lesser gender.

Hard science has reached an entirely different conclusion. Namely, the modern human brain is an entire radio and TV station—creating, sending and receiving information. Neuroscientists tell us that the female hominid brain is not just a radio receiver designed to take delivery of messages from an alleged male superior as alleged by some rabid religionists. Why then does she so often play a role as if needing direction? **IF** she is indeed the superior one, why does she, seemly so often, act in inferior ways? Empirical evidence available in this day of MRIs and SPECT brain scans affirms the sending and receiving design. Then why are over half of the world's men and women still stuck in ancient mythological belief processes wherein divine messages are received and then interpreted by a select male few? It appears to be accepted as true worldwide, that women in particular, must receive orders and certainty from somewhere other than their own brain perceptions.

The unchanging status of women in most of the world suggests something other than physical, cultural and economic constraints have been, and still are, impinging on women's abilities to access and demonstrate their superior abilities.

Compounding the observable limitations on modern women, other subtler dynamics are apparently at work. Even in the progressive U.S. culture, many still accept the stereotypical separation of girls and boys into math vs. reading categories. Social scientists have presented evidence showing how untenable this belief is, and yet it is still held forth as fact. Why? Because there is also evidence to support the idea. For example, when girls are reminded of their gender before a math test, even by something as benign as a Male/Female "check box" at the top of the test, their math scores decline when compared to their male counterparts. What is it about expectation and self-evaluation that would compel the world's female population to adopt this stance? (4)

The following is an example of female negative self-evaluation. Among economically disadvantaged urban girls between the ages of 10 and 13, as they experience natural physical development, begin to behave as if they carry a sizeable sign on their back saying PREY. As these self-defined bottom rung girls begin to develop hips and breasts, older boys commence making suggestive remarks. Many of these girls, frequently uneducated, immature and naïve, feel at a loss and panicky when confronted by males of any age. Most are without mentors or support groups. They unconsciously learn to become victims. In Eastern and Middle-eastern cultures, pre-pubescent girls can literally be bargained for like so much meat. Within these cultures it is little wonder females in general appear to act and feel so inferior.

How does it happen that in every major culture there is a fundamental assumption that men are naturally superior? When compared to their female counterparts recent research suggests that men are expected to be successful in a public arena and have a fulfilled personal life. For women, author Sheryl Sandberg (5) suggests the expectation is almost reversed. "Attempting to be successful is doomed to failure."

Warnings of potential failure for women abound in every echelon of life; workingwomen, exhausted from three or four jobs, hit the aforementioned glass ceiling with no promotion in sight. Then, while working even harder, not surprisingly something gives. The time-honored message to women is she must give up something and it must be the best choice for her family and everyone involved. "No one can do it all." Right? Most of the time in the U.S. the popular conclusion would tell us that what she gives up should obviously be her out of the house employment.

All over the world the proverbial refrain is heard, no sane person would choose to work over what traditionalists call a regular life. Or the familiar, "I don't know how she does it all!" While considered a compliment, it is good for only so many motivational laurels. Women quickly discover the popularized certainty, no one can do it all, is indeed true. Finally she gives up and in to the celebrated truth, which really says, no woman should do it all.

While according to Sandberg, repeated tallies reveal that female scores on every known comparison test are equal to or higher than her male analog; women in general deny such results. Sandberg suggests that women can't seem to shake the feeling that somehow the test scores and their successes in the marketplace are fraudulent, that it is only a matter of time until they are discovered to be impostors with lucky scores and limited abilities. When men are asked to offer an explanation of their success, they credit their own innate skills. When women are asked, they attribute their success to working really hard or being just plain lucky.

Not too long ago, as a part of writing *Woman Aware*, I interviewed several women who have been dazzlingly successful in their so-called competition with talented men. During my conversation with a prominent surgeon in the Palm Springs area, she revealed a couple of important lessons learned while growing up in the shadow of her renowned surgeon father. One: if she could possibly be content in any other field of medicine besides surgery, she should do it. Why? Number two: Because the field is dominated by males who judge their own performance as better than it actually is while women do the opposite. Recent research has validated this idea. Assessments, published in the *Journal of Surgical Research* of students in a surgery rotation, found that when asked to evaluate themselves, the female students gave themselves lower scores than the male students despite faculty evaluations showing the female surgeons out-performed the men. (6)

There are a couple of observable influences that may have a significant bearing, consciously and unconsciously, on the personality and attitudinal differences of the female gender. Male *Homo sapiens*, along with a large segment of the animal kingdom, evolved brute strength as their key contribution to the continued existence of their species. Evolution undoubtedly facilitated this to insure the survival of offspring. Physical strength still allows for male dominance in most of today's more undeveloped societies. However, when a society evolves beyond interactions requiring mere brute strength, the need for male dominance diminishes or even becomes nonexistent.

One of the most highly developed ancient civilizations was Egypt. Recovered hieroglyphics reveal that under Egyptian law, women were the equals of men. They could (1.) Own land. (2.) Own and manage commercial property. (3.) Represent themselves in court cases. They could also sit on juries, testify in trials, initiate lawsuits and recover assets of their household. Remember these successful gender equivalencies in this acknowledged advanced society existed 3000 years before the American suffrage heroine Susan B. Anthony was born.

Things did not always proceed in an ideal fashion in ancient Egypt. Divorce did exist but equivalency of genders was at the heart of it. Divorce could begin on the initiative of either spouse. A divorced status did not prevent women from remarrying, as shown by the archaeological data.

Egyptian texts further declared, "In the beginning there was Isis, Oldest of the Old. She was the Goddess from whom all beginning arose." Isis ruled Egypt with her husband Osiris whose mythical regenerative powers allowed the Nile to overflow annually. Her legendary story centers on the death and resurrection of her beloved spouse. When Osiris as killed, Isis wandered the lands looking for the corpse, which she then, by the first rite of mummification, restores to eternal life and conceives their son Horus. Thus, the mythical counterpart, the pharaoh, succeeds the father and insures the continuity of life. This myth represents the God who must be sacrificed in order to insure renewal, which in turn becomes the death and resurrection story later absorbed into the Christian sacred story. Over a thousand years after the Isis narrative, the Hebrew worshippers of Yahweh asserted that it was a male, rather than a female, who created the world. One must wonder what happened to the Goddess? (7) For an answer we return to the ancient record that most Westerners are accustomed to reviewing: The Old Testament Scriptures. In these writings we may discover how gender regression occurred. Or why Western and Mid-Eastern worlds constructed male dominated societies after Egypt had set such a remarkable example of gender equality.

The Hebrew creation story asserts that even modern women must still pay for Eve's alleged sins. We know from cultural anthropologists that the first gods were women who dominated societies and their religions for many thousands of years. We conclude that the mythical stories of divine male deities seizing power were a reflection of the contemporary social climate as men began seizing of power on earth. This became known as the Patriarchal system and has been in existence for a little over three thousand years. As men assumed political and economic power on earth, *otherworld* theological beliefs changed. One of the daily prayers of Hebrew males begins with: "Blessed Art Thou O Lord our God ... who has not made me a woman."

During the first century (CE), the Christian writer St. Paul said, "Let the woman learn in silence with all subjection ... For Adam was first formed ... and was

Woman Aware

not deceived but the woman being deceived was in the transgression." I must ask: If Adam was made in the image of an omniscient God, why didn't he prevent Eve's alleged mistake?

A little later in the seventh century (CE), the Islamic prophet Mohamed said, "When Eve was created, Satan rejoiced." The fact is, the idea of female subjugation and male domination is inherent in the basic theological structure of our three most popular modern-day religious systems. Within The Big Three, males rule!

In ancient Egypt the Goddess was central in their worship ceremony. Brute strength, on the part of the Egyptian populace, was not well regarded and was considered, for the most part, unnecessary. The result, women participated in the furthering of Egypt as the most advanced civilization of the ancient world. In most places where male domination was and still is revered and accepted as primary, the culture remains backward and under developed.

As the decades moved on, the status and position of women continued to lose ground. The principal religious leaders and their believers held fast to their idea of the construction of a worldwide male dominated society. They insisted that it was God's creation decree that women were to be regarded as gratuitous, carnal creatures. This male proclamation became a theological dictum. The accepted truth of the Eden myth proved that women were the source of evil on this planet, as every faithful follower knows and, of course, each word of this God-given sacred scriptural writing must be taken literally. (8)

The Egyptian civilization had long before laid aside the brute strength domination by the male. We may read in the scriptures adopted by all of The Big Three religions, about an Egyptian woman betraying the Hebrew iconic leader, Joseph. The repeated re-telling of this story undoubtedly had its influence on the Hebrew developers of later theology and political philosophy. If, as the Old Testament scriptural story would have us understand, the influence of a woman could result in 400 years of slavery for the entire Hebrew clan, it seems little wonder that Joseph's Hebrew heirs elected patriarchal leadership and male dominance in reaction! In the same scriptures we find the Hebrew patriarchal leaders assuming a pose of contempt for women. Continuing the sacred visions and revelations they use their scriptural writings to lock women into the role of a passive and inferior being who progressively becomes the controlled property of man. The revered Old Testament scriptures appear to be carefully designed to suppress the earlier Egyptian cultural arrangement of gender equivalency. Moses is reported to have created the myth of the Genesis and the tale of Adam and Eve so that his writings were seen to be deified proof that man was created to hold the ultimate power. The status of the Divine Male became the status of the mortal male. It is not an accident that the Levite priests and the Hebrew deity Yahweh were on the same page, as far as male dominance was concerned. Select passages proved this truth and several other, rather more uncomfortable, doctrines beyond a doubt.

Recent attempts to restructure the Hebrew religion in the context of modern evidence resulted in obvious conflicts between the biblical story and archeological evidence. W. Dever, the eminent archeologist, stated, unequivocally, "Many of the biblical texts are both late and elitist, and thus may constitute less direct evidence of the actual early (Hebrew) cult practice than archeological discoveries." (9) The early authors of biblical writings obviously sought to impose their views of a new monotheistic deity thus revising the earlier worldview. The inclination to select data favoring their own theology did not differ from other writers of the ancient world or the second century (CE) authors of the Christian canon, but in both cases their old scriptural works were not based on actual objective history.

The next chapter will convey this ancient story in more detail. The writings that most Westerners refer to as the sacred Old Testament scriptures, whether or not true in all the details, reveal the gradual subservience imposed on women after the fabled Exodus from Egypt. It is clear that these scriptural writings have impacted gender equivalency in our Western world.

CHAPTER 6

The Hebrew Chronicles

The Old Testament scriptural storyline involves a number of archetypal narratives. These ancient Eastern world tales consciously and unconsciously influence our modern Western world beliefs. The well-known Hebrew tale of a worldwide flood, sent to punish evildoers, was borrowed from part of an even older legend. What many in the West do not realize is that this flood tale was a part of the ancient Epic of Gilgamesh (1) and far older than any of the Greek, Hebrew or other well-known legends of the flood. Gilgamesh was the hero king of ancient Samaria who, while on an epic pilgrimage, met a very old man named Utnapashtim. He was told the story of how the gods, many centuries before, were so angry with humans that they sent a great flood. Fortunately, one of the gods pre-warned Utnapashtim. He was then also instructed to fabricate a huge boat into which he would take the "seed of all existing creatures." The flood destroyed all living things and when the vessel finally came to rest on a mountaintop, one of the gods sent a rainbow as a gesture that no more floods would be wrought. Does this myth sound familiar?

In their flood tale the ancient Sumerians had already accounted for the dispersal of people around the Mediterranean world. The Hebrews added a slightly different twist to the flood perspective. Their retelling of the legend gave it a slightly more identifiable cultural bent. In their eloquent version, the Hebrew clan becomes Jehovah's chosen people. This lends a personalized thread to the story. Their singular, omnipotent God selected them to be His earthly experiment. Some other details embellished the legend to localize it, possibly to make it more believable to the Hebrew Yahweh followers. After the flood receded, some of the survivors went north and built a town called Nineveh. Another group settled near the Nile and became the Egyptians. Abraham is said to have "moved his tent" to a distant desert area and as an old man, by means of one of his young slave girls, produced a son named Ishmael. Thirteen years later as a really, really old man (100+), Abraham produced an heir with his wife Sarah, who, according to this story, was 91 years old. Resentment and jealousy may have bested poor old Sarah because she banished her "wild–man" stepson Ishmael and his slave girl Mother to a remote part of the desert. According to the Hebrew story, Ishmael became the progenitor of the desert religion Muslims.

In the history of Western civilization, biblical scholars initially assumed the patriarchs and matriarchs of the Old Testament scriptures were a believable composite of people living in the 2nd millennium BCE. As new archeological evidence began to emerge, new conclusions about the revered texts also followed.

Based on prevailing archaeology, (2) as well as ancient texts, the modern point of view is that no persuasive evidence points to the patriarchs living in the 2nd millennium but rather the Old Testament biblical texts more accurately describe 1st millennium circumstances and concerns. As E. Gadon has said in her soundly researched book, "From an archeological perspective the early history of the Hebrew people is murky. No material evidence has been found to corroborate the legendary accounts of the Patriarchs, either the Egyptian Exodus, or the long sojourn in the Sinai desert." (3)

William Dever has also suggested that by the last quarter of the 20th century, "most respectable archaeologists had given up any hope of recovering an evidential context that would make Abraham, Isaac or Jacob credible historical figures." It was concluded that the fantastic Old Testament stories were fabricated to pass on cultural and religious values from one generation to the next. The oral tradition worked really well in terms of Hebrew clan cohesiveness. Historical facts became jumbled; events and characters were created to serve the beliefs of Hebrew leaders, especially the Levitical priests. As the oral traditions gradually infused their written tradition, myths came to be regarded as quasi-historical accounts. Two of the many creation myths (Genesis one and two) were included as literal occurrences. The eloquent Hebrew storytellers always connected their narratives to their Hebrew tribe, thus identifying Yahweh's chosen, as themselves!

Turning to the Old Testament stories that have influenced Western Civilization's modern perspective, we find that just down the family line, Abraham's great grandson, "coat of many colors" Joseph, was kidnapped by his jealous brothers and sold into slavery in Egypt. He found himself in the household of a wealthy officer in the Pharaoh's service.

By dint of hard work and his own intelligence, Joseph rose through the ranks of the household slaves, eventually becoming the overseer of the household estates. Under Joseph's supervision everything ran smoothly, and the wealthy Egyptian bureaucrat, Potiphar was free to devote himself to his great passion, food, perhaps a subtle suggestion that Potiphar's sexual prowess was not all it should have been. The biblical story suggests that his Egyptian wife, assuming a role not unlike Mrs. Robinson, [4] *"Cast her eyes on Joseph and said, Lie with me."* She was probably a lonely, bored woman thrown into the company of an unusually handsome, attractive man. (The Channing Tatum of the Egyptian world?) Joseph was said to have rebuffed her but unfortunately she snagged his loincloth as he fled. She called her household staff and told her version of near rape claiming that only her screams had rebuffed his sexual advances. When her husband returned home, she repeated the same tall tale.

Potiphar's dilemma: Should he hold on to a beneficial servant, or should he believe his wife and punish Joseph? He chose the latter course of action, possibly compelled by the fact that the Egyptian law of divorce would probably grant half of his possessions to his wife. He charged Joseph and put him in prison. Eventually Joseph was paroled, and according to the story, his original Hebrew clan had begun to multiply exponentially. Remember, it all started with a woman's false accusations.

After viewing the cultural and civil advances made by Egypt, it is with no little surprise that we become impressed, even shocked, by the obvious impact Hebrew storytelling has had on Western culture. Comparing Egyptian society, laws, and philosophy along with the equality of genders, it is apparent that Western cultures took a step backwards as they looked to the brute strength of the Hebrew God, Yahweh, to represent the idealized deity to worship.

IF Egyptians, as a model society were so advanced, why would self-styled progressive civilizations later decide to take this backward step? Why was the West so receptive to the primitive Hebrew male supremacy point of view? With Idealized male gods and a patriarchal social system it was a culturally regressive move. The male dominated historical world of the Middle East was and still is a primitive culture in terms of laws, justice, and gender equality, particularly in comparison to ancient Egypt.

According to oral tradition, the Hebrew clans were made slaves in Egypt. Then Moses stepped forward and led an Exodus, which was under the reputed direction of an omniscient, pissed off and all-powerful male god named Yahweh. These exit tales, recounted by priests and their scribes, became the central core of Hebrew philosophy and history.

However, unless we re-name the nomadic Hebrew clan or reinvent the narrative, it appears that the renowned Exodus of the Hebrews was so insignificant in the larger and well-documented history of the time; it went virtually unnoticed and unremarked in the secular literature of the day. (5) Although the contemporary recorded history is quite voluminous, no scribe or historian of that day mentions the momentous exit as recorded in the Hebrew Old Testament scriptures. Contemporary secular records of the Hebrew exodus and the subsequent conquest of the "milk and honey lands" are virtually unknown. Modern archeological records of ancient happenings are mysteriously missing. What little archeological material is available contradicts the Hebrew scriptural records. Apparently this band of nomads was overlooked by the ample history of their time. They were in all likelihood an inconsequential ragtag group milling around the upper regions of the Sinai Desert too inconspicuous for the historians of the time to notice.

The desire of this nomadic desert tribe to enshrine and then preserve the dominance of a patriarchal system with their singular male God was most likely in reaction to survival needs and, perhaps, the repeated narrative of Joseph's subservience under female domination in Egypt. Certainly, these larger-than-life stories would make powerful and lasting impressions on future Hebrew generations. (6)

The single mention of an Israeli clan as a people who lived in the Judean foothills at roughly the same time (1200 BCE) was on a Pharaoh Merneptah victory stele. (7) Touting "Israel is laid waste; and seed is no more," it was considered a singularly important discovery because it is the only mention of Israel. Apparently the Egyptian pharaoh wanted to make sure the entire Sinai desert land was under his dominion. When the Hebrew desert clan finally settled down, the clan had two things going for them: First, they were not only defeated but without seed for planting, thus they were not likely to become an imminent threat. They were left without a future in their newly conquered Israeli lands, an unimpressive 150 miles in length and about 50 miles across. Their "land of milk and honey" was, for the most part, a monotonous terrain of dry desert. Hebrew history, when viewed with unbiased eyes, amounts to little more than a few colorful yarns about battles in which an all-powerful, jealous male God delivered them victories over a few desert rural villages, in spite of their faithlessness and ineptitude. Second, as nomads they were still dependent on male brute strength for basic survival in an inhospitable desert terrain. As tent dwellers, they had little interest in monolithic walls or temples on which to inscribe and preserve their tribal tale. They were magnificent storytellers! They carried these oral chronicles with them as word-of-mouth legends. The stories were told and retold becoming the colorful cohesive thread that held their cultural identity together prior to the advent of scriptures, principally the Torah, first five books of the Old Testament, and the hero-legends of their nomad prophets. These were copied over and over and, when eventually bound together as books, supplanted the need for priests as storytellers.

The basic scriptural admonition was: 1. Never question priestly authority. 2. Accept whatever the priestly rants say about a jealous, vicious god who annihilates whole villages of women and children because they were not his chosen people. Just believe rather than think.

This is reminiscent of a later (7th Century CE) desert wanderer who, after holing up in a cave, had epiphanies that demanded his followers kill the infidel (Quran 4/89) non-believers. (8)

It was not until about 150 CE that the story of Jesus the rabbi Christ was retold enough times that the older scriptural narratives of the Hebrew prophets began to be referenced and revered by the growing Christian world. By the third or fourth century CE, it was decided by early Christian church leaders in Rome that there was enough significant scriptural verbiage that could be interpreted as messianic prophecies in the Old Testament scriptures. These messianic prophecies were thought to validate its existence within the contended Christian written liturgy. By the third century, early Christian church fathers asserted that the two Hebrew creation stories plus the passages that seemed to foretell the coming of the Messiah, in the form of Jesus the Christ, were the true purpose of the Old Hebrew scriptures. Thus, many of the old manuscript scriptures were laid beside the more recently fashioned New Testament scrolls to form the new Bible scriptures for Christians. The Church leaders made sure that male power dominated. Major doctrines emphasized an all-powerful Male as the one and only one true God with no partner, no companion, no associate, and no equal. Males on earth became the absolute authority. Select scriptures were selected to support this assertion. Hebrew clan leaders, Christian church fathers and later the Pope, left no room in their theology for gender equality.

While a few scholars dispute that Jesus and his disciples actually existed, others accept the historical existence of a first century rabbi named Jesus of Nazareth. A few hundred years before the appearance of Jesus, this same Hebrew clan had taken on the designation *Jew* to distinguish their religious affiliation to Jehovah and the Temple at Jerusalem. In other words, the term Jew did not come into existence until hundreds of years after the story of the Exodus and then it referred to a religious affiliation, not a nationality or race. Therefore, there never was a Jewish Exodus, Jewish Passover or a Jewish Torah. These were all productions of the Hebrews.

Then we come to St Paul, (9) a rather radical religious follower, who sealed the male dominance theme with his letters to the various early churches. To Timothy he is said to have written, "Let women keep silent because they were created second, and sinned first." Either Paul was an unmitigated misogynist or Church history has left out the egalitarian view of genders as taught by Jesus. Even Paul suggested a superior democratic point of view in his epistle to the Galatians 3:27-8: "For as many of you as were baptized into Christ have put on Christ. There is neither Jew nor Greek, there is neither slave nor free, there is neither male nor female, for you are all one in Christ Jesus." The membership ritual of baptism offered the suspension of the various inequalities existing between socio-economic, sexual and political affiliations. These were to be suspended in the new religion, then being called Christianity.

In fact, something altogether opposite happened in the generation following Paul, aside from the prosecution/persecution issue. (10) The Christian churches that looked to Paul as their founder became divided on teachings about women's role. Some groups in these second-generation Pauline churches continued to expand the view that gender hierarchy was overcome through baptism. In Christ there was no more male and female. This also meant that "born again" Christians should transcend marital relations and gender issues. These Pauline Christians wrote scriptural texts, such as the Acts of Paul and Thecla, which celebrates the story of a woman converted by St. Paul who rejects her fiancé, adopts men's clothing, and travels as an evangelist. Persecuted by the agents of the state, she is vindicated by God through miraculous protection from harm. Paul reappears at the end of the story to affirm her role and commission her to preach in her hometown. (11)

In 313 CE, the newly converted Christian Emperor, Constantine ordered fifty copies of the existing compendium scriptures to be distributed throughout the empire. He then baptized his entire army by marching them through a river. Thus, the emperor declared the entire Roman world Christian, which as a philosophy has influenced Western culture and women's position as nothing else before or after!

CHAPTER 7

Unconscious Influences

It is particularly important that women today see how unconscious motivators have affected their gender status in almost every culture on earth. While Freud is often given credit for the invention of the word *unconscious*, meaning processes of the human brain that occur automatically without awareness and yet impact behavior and mind processes, it was in use before Freud or psychoanalysis was invented. Freud certainly popularized the word during the rise of his psychoanalytic treatment and his notorious Victorian attitude toward women. In his mind, women were singular possessors of Hysteria, literally *movement of the womb.* His treatments of alleged female mental aberrations like Hysteria, probably set the social progress of women back at least a hundred years. The term unconscious was in use earlier, and was most likely invented by the German philosopher Friedrich Schelling (1) and later found in the poetry of the American Samuel Coleridge. Unconscious influences impacting cultures and especially modern women, is central to this book *Woman Aware*.

Robert Milton Ph.D.

Freud compared himself to an archaeologist, excavating layers of the human mind. He also proposed the analogy of the iceberg, in that just the barest tip, i.e. consciousness, breaches the surface of awareness whereas the enormous and, perhaps, "dangerous and/or innovative" part remains unexposed below the surface. To make the unconscious conscious was the understood work of psychoanalysis. It is certainly one of the challenges of the book you are now reading.

Even State governments are recognizing unconscious influences that smack us with silly but important unconscious insinuations. As a part of an endeavor to purge legal statutes of such unconscious gender bias, bills are being passed in various American States that are going into effect even as you read this. No small task, changing "fisherman" into "fisher" or "penmanship" into "handwriting." From now on, in many states' statutes, "his" will be "his and hers" and "clergyman" will be seen as "clergy". Why? Because our vocabulary words really do matter and continue to impact the human unconscious. Many educators today are suggesting that it is anachronistic to continue the use of male-generic-based language as if it is the singular all-inclusive structure of the human language. The modern dictionary defines Mankind as the human race ... taken collectively. The same modern dictionary defines Womankind as women taken collectively. The State legislators are correct; a change in language structure is absolutely necessary.

While most of us as adults may be so accustomed to seeing and reading the male biased verbiage, it is difficult to appreciate their unconscious impact on today's more literate societies. Studies have demonstrated that words and symbols do have an impact, especially on children. For example, as cited in a previous chapter, **IF** scores are lowered for seven year-old girls on a math test by simply checking a box that defines the test-taker as female, how many other unconscious motivators are affecting children as they move toward adulthood? As Sheryl Sandberg pointed out, if grown men typically overestimate their abilities while women underestimate theirs, it would seem important for us to understand when and why subliminal forces influence both men and women.

If you Google *parenting* you'll locate more than 50,000 books advertising the dos and don'ts for properly rearing children. Many of these suggest that early childhood experiences, particularly when presented in some subliminal manner, will change the ultimate outcome of a child's life. In fact, in 2012 researchers for the *American Association for the Advancement of Science* came together to share their investigations on how early un-remembered experiences actually wire our brains and bodies to succeed or struggle in later life. (2)

Judith Harris presents a slightly contrasting view in her controversial prize-winning book *The Nurture Assumption.* (3) It seems to assail every tenet of traditional psychological child development. She advocates that usual parenting techniques have little influence on a child's development as they approach adulthood. Instead, her research suggests that it is the child's adolescent peer group that makes the greatest impact. Here again, her investigations suggest that it is most likely unconscious influences during adolescence that have the most weight. She proposes that its not the parental do-s and don'ts that are making the impact but rather the subtle subliminal messages of adolescence that impact personality, gender behavior, and the *who* children eventually become as adults.

In the 1950's, a psychologist named Harry Harlow [4] at the University of Wisconsin performed a series of disquieting experiments on baby monkeys. He separated the babies from their mothers and presented them with wire moms where food was available and terrycloth moms where texture and warmth was available. The monkeys, who were isolated with just the wire mom and food, grew up traumatized.

When they were finally removed from isolation, many went into a "state of emotional shock," Harlow reported. Some refused food and just clutched and rocked. They did not play with other monkeys and could not form relationships with their peers. "Twelve months of isolation almost obliterated the animals social abilities," wrote Harlow. Some of the terrycloth mom monkeys fared slightly better in that a few did, at a later date, form relationships.

Psychologist Harlow's disturbing research may be fraught with ethical disapproval, and it is impossible to imagine thinking about performing similar experiments on human subjects. But, heartbreakingly, millions of children are battered, abandoned, or lose their parents to violence or disease and become similar unwitting subjects in just such Harlow-esque experimental trials. Thousands are raised in inadequately staffed institutions where they obtain minimum stimulus, follow a fixed schedule, and don't get empathetic care. Such children characteristically have lower IQ scores than their peers, growth is stunted, and they struggle with verbal communication, social behavior, and forming attachments.

It is perhaps easy for us to recognize the factors that changed these children's lives; physical abuse and deprivation are rather obvious as point-at-able causes of later emotional or mental aberrations. Most unconscious child abuses are not so easy to identify or prohibit.

Richard Dawkins (5) put it in the form of a commonplace narrative often seen at the Christmas season in London: Three children are typically dressed up as the wise men. The accompanying story labels one child Muslim, another Hindu and the third Christian; what may be considered "child abuse" is the fact that these thusly labeled children were all four years old. Question: How can any thinking adult describe a pre-school child as a Muslim, Christian or Hindu? Would the same adults tag these same children economic monetarist, neo-isolationist or liberal Republican? Most thinking adults will consider labels regarding political or economic jargon to be for them to decide, after they have grown up.

But in the provisos of the book you are now reading, religious brand names are a cultural exception. Religious labels in the cultures of The Big Three are tacked on children without a moment's hesitation or serious thought. That parents, teachers and neighbors should agree on this for pre-school children is a form of child exploitation. There is an unconscious, almost absolute, agreement within these cultures that their children should be indoctrinated as early as possible to make sure their beliefs match adult expectations. Talk about child abuse! How different religious education might be, especially for girls, if children were offered the possibility of considering the holistic vision of human life that empirical research has to offer. If we can become aware the amazing view of the universe science has to offer, we will undoubtedly experience a different outcome. If we compare the various myths that have impacted the human species, especially girls, we will begin to see how very biased a culture can be in its unconscious influence of genders. As Dawkins remarked, "poetic inspiration far outclasses any of the mutually contradictory faiths and disappointingly recent traditions of the world's religions."

You may ask "what about grown-ups? Aren't adults, particularly men, less susceptible to unconscious stimuli? Perhaps not, consider this simple illustration of unconscious conditioning. In the men's washroom at the Schiphol Airport in Amsterdam men see a common housefly in the urinal. Men do their best to wash it down the drain but fail. They give up, figuring the fly has been super glued. Amsterdam airport urinals would pass inspection in a hospital surgical room, but no one notices. Why? What they do notice is a housefly near the drain. But if you were to look harder you would see the fly is etched into the porcelain. Because researchers found it improves the aim of males! If a man sees the fly, he aims at it. Studies have shown that housefly etchings improve spillage by 80%. Unconscious influences in this case obviously do spillover into a man's brain!

For most of human history only the concepts of conscious thought and intentional behavior existed. In the 1800s, two very different developments, experiments with hypnotism and Darwin's evolution ideas, both pointed to the possibility of unconscious or unintended causes in human behavior. For an example we turn to current events. Recent research has uncovered data that reveals unconscious influences determine some charitable donations. People named Kim or Ken are more likely to donate to victims of Hurricane Katrina, while Rons and Rachels give to the cause of Hurricane Rita more generously. Apparently our world is populated with words and images that prompt unexpected, unconscious decisions. We are so deeply, and unconsciously, attracted to our own initials that we give more willingly to the victims of hurricanes that begin with the same letters as our names!

It is well known that our human brain (male and female) is fantastically complex, having within modern times, engineered space travel, created telescopes that look back in time billions of years, and liberated nuclear energy. Actually, it seems little wonder that we are unconsciously influenced by our surroundings. It may still be harder to imagine that you are more likely to solve puzzles if you watch an illuminated light bulb. Studies found that viewing a picture of a light bulb inspires creative thinking, apparently because in our culture the illuminated light bulb symbolizes insight. This, too, was born out by a recent study about unconscious influences.

Social interactions also have effects on the unconscious. Professional bicyclists pedal faster when there are watching bystanders. When a picture of two eyes was hung on the wall where teachers who took tea in the break room at Newcastle University, it was discovered that they contributed 300 percent more to a cash box. Apparently we are unconsciously sensitive to human surveillance, so we behave more nobly if we're watched, if only by a photograph.

The physical environment, from location to color, also guides our hand in subliminal ways. Dimly lit interiors metaphorically imply no one's watching and encourage dishonesty and theft, while even blue lights discourage crime because they're associated with the police. Further data revealed that Olympic judo athletes are more likely to win when they wear red because evidently red makes them behave more aggressively and referees tend to see them as winners. (6)

According to Daniel Dennett, (7) in the natural sciences, especially neurobiology, the assumption of *conscious primacy* is not nearly as prevalent as once thought. Dennett suggests an alternative perspective, in which the "unconscious is minding the store when the owner is absent," is now generally accepted. We can no longer assume that singular conscious processes drive complex behavior in living things, particularly human beings. Instead, it must be acknowledged that adaptive unconscious processes that accrued through natural selection are in charge. It is not that consciousness plays no role; it's that consciousness is no longer considered essential to achieve the adaptive, behavioral guidance demonstrated in emerging empirical research. Unconscious processes are elegant as well as adaptive throughout the living world. Within human nature, the unconscious mind is the rule, not the exception.

Recently it has been found that even under stressful conditions, or perhaps because of stress, the unconscious plays a major role in facilitating human success and survival. Neuro-scientists discovered that whenever human beings must acquire and hold new knowledge under stress, the human brain deploys unconscious rather than conscious learning processes. The switch from conscious to unconscious systems is triggered by mineral corticoid receptors. Hormones released in response to stress by the adrenal cortex activate these receptors. (8) Evidence of this type suggests that our unconscious mind is the rule, not the exception! In the next chapter we will see how the unconscious has publically and privately influenced the behavior of modern women the world over.

CHAPTER 8

The Newly Conscious Woman

The anti-feminist rants found in any of The Big Three scriptural documents could result in most modern women perceiving their gender as disposable. In the sacred writings of church hierarchies, including Hebrew, Evangelical and Desert religions, women are considered footnotes, a traditionally accepted omniscient afterthought. The male god, Jehovah/God/Allah, made women from man's rib on the sixth day of creation. In addition, each of The Big Three blame women for being responsible for the introduction of sin, particularly if nakedness and sex are included as sinful.

In today's reality, notwithstanding ancient scriptural documentation, The Big Three religions are gradually cutting back their overt banishment of women. Why? The female gender is absolutely critical to the not-so-subtle schemes of church leaders and their procreative ambitions to increase membership. Increased birthrate assumes increased membership. Nearly a decade ago San Franciscan Richard Rodriquez [1] wrote about the plight of gay men and their much-publicized exclusion from The Big Three. He could have just as easily been writing about today's women's sideline attendance at one of these churches.

Recent actuaries suggest that young, progressive women of industrialized countries are becoming reticent to present their babies to the Western church for the various rites of membership. Even though for past centuries women have sustained most of the ecclesiastical systems, particularly The Big Three, solely by the birthrates of female members. This statistic has changed. Following the recent pedophile scandals in the Christian world, the Muslim demand for Sharia law, and Jewish demands for a return to Hebrew traditions, coupled with the influence of higher education, the inclination to blindly follow traditional ecclesiastic demand is reversing.

One exception to this worldwide tendency is the archaic insistence made by certain desert religions that women remain in male custody as virtual slaves. Statistics suggest that in recent decades the church systems need women more than women need the churches. When the women of the desert religions discover this piece of information, their freedom from male domination and slavery will be made possible and visible. Acknowledgement of this fact can be found in the recent modification of doctrines that had in previous eras banished women from holding office in both the Jewish and Christian systems. However, progress is very slow, because as Rodriquez suggests, in all three, Jew, Christian or Muslim, when their Holy Scripture is quoted, "the default gender setting has been and continues to be HE."

While some modernists may insist that God is spirit or the "I am that I am," is without gender specificity, and that YAHWEH is unnamable or that ALLAH means the greatest, without reference to gender, most still refer to HE when referencing the currently popular deities. In fact, consciously and unconsciously according to popular polls, our world populations, church going or not, have been trained, consciously and unconsciously, to believe that the great Oneness is male.

In spite of this male emphasis, it also seems clear that in some parts of the world, attitudes toward women are slowly but surely shifting. In countries described as progressive or industrialized, opinion polls as well as secular courts are providing data in favor of woman's rights, which is certainly in keeping with a more natural historical order in progressive civilizations. Apart from the desert religions, with their backward facing dogmas, change is slowly happening in the world at large. The Muslim apprehension regarding this change is not because females are unclear regarding divinely delivered scriptures but rather the exact opposite. This book suggests that Islam will shortly be tested with a new kind of Arab Spring, and because it is so late in coming it will be more like a female Arab Autumn. With technology and the worldwide web serving up informational connections, it will happen. As women reevaluate their own aptitudes, these religion-based cultures must also acknowledge the *Woman Aware*. She is becoming aware of her real, and needful, place within their social order. When The Big Three are able to perceive the female gender as "the greatest" and indistinguishable from "the greatest," as singularly male, it will happen! The great I AM, more accurately translated, as *bringing into being*, can no longer be called exclusively male. In fact, a precise definition portrays naissance. I AM more accurately refers to the birthing process by the female gender. With or without the acceptance of these realities, the Arab Autumn will happen.

The world at large, must also accept similar changes. The majority of women are now living without spouses. (2) That tabulation advocates for boys in growing up with the obvious understanding and appreciation that women are autonomous and strong. The prospect of a generation of children being raised by women in homes without fathers is challenging for religious institutions whose crucial notion of deity is Father or Abba. A woman who can do without a husband can do without any patriarchal authority. As Rodriquez points out, the modern single mother may well be the greatest single threat to the patriarchal determinates of The Big Three religions. The ecclesiastic old guard must realize that *bringing into being* or naissance are not words that any religion should christen male only. When they do realize, they will be able to appreciate the importance and true value of women.

Keeping women and their children dependent on male support may be why the desert religions advocated plural marriages in the first place. If women were left alone they probably could have demonstrated their independence eons ago. (3) The recent spike in divorce rates the world over suggests at the very least, women in general, are not happy with the interactions and potential long-term relationships they have with men. Since recent statistics reveal that the majority of women in democratic countries are living without husbands, the realization that a woman can do without a husband also implies that women can do without patriarchal church authority. This includes ecclesiastic determinism with male gender as its ideal. For example, the majority of boys growing up in America will probably now begin to assume that women, their mothers, are strong and can get along perfectly fine without male dominance. Unfortunately, this also indicates that they may grow up without a model of male playfulness or male compassion.

If we continue to embrace The Big Three and their traditional adherence, in one form or another, to the Hebrew God *Yahweh,* we will continue to embrace the singular male god as the ideal all humans must attempt to emulate. The unconscious message washes over every child's brain: God is male; if I am male I can be like a god, if I am female I will never measure up. Think about it. In every nation on this globe the message from birth onward is that God is male and the unconscious message is males are supreme and superior and in control. Males rule and pass judgment.

Here I would like to introduce a dramatic story that actually happened in Sweden: (4)

In 1973, two gun-toting felons entered a Stockholm bank and terrified bank employees with threats and the actual firing of their machine guns. The would-be bank robbers held the police at bay with four hostages for five days. After their rescue, the hostages who had been abused, strapped with dynamite and confined to the bank vault, exhibited positive support for their captors! The hostages actually began to feel that their captors were defending them from the police. One of the women actually became engaged to marry one of the robbers. Another built up a 'defense fund' to help pay for lawyers. Without a doubt this weird behavior suggested a deep emotional bonding with their controlling captors.

Thus the <u>Stockholm Syndrome</u> came into being.

When a child's normally developing imagination is subordinated to the memorization of authoritative God texts, unconscious forces are at work. When demands for obedience to a supreme and superior male god are introduced and advocated to children, their minds are affected and infected. When little girls are conditioned to believe that males rule and pass judgment, then unconscious forces take over that can be likened to those feelings known as the Stockholm syndrome *(SS)*. It's as if every little girl is a sufferer of the syndrome where, as victims, they emotionally bond to their supreme controller. They must then offer themselves in support of the father-god. It is the female's primary survival strategy. In some cases, female victims of intimidation, abuse, and even rape may years later describe their subjugator as a "great person."

It is important to remember that the Stockholm syndrome develops unconsciously on an involuntary basis. The behavioral strategy is a survival instinct that develops as an attempt to live in the context of perceived threats and/or the controlling environment. Why women in almost every culture accept submissive and compliant roles can be explained in part by this dynamic syndrome.

To maintain potential anxiety and fear for years is much too damaging to the human psyche, so the human mind tells itself mythical fairy tales about hope and contentment to safeguard itself. That is the essence of the Stockholm syndrome as well as the male dominated religions. Religions that teach their initiates that failure to please God or failure to perform ecclesiastic rituals will result in punishment or even death or hell-fire can be compared to the Stockholm felons. "Good people can do good things and bad people can do bad things, but for good people to do bad things—that takes religion." (5)

As a hostage in a robbery, threatened by machine guns, it is easy to understand the perceived inability to get away. In religious relationships the belief that one cannot escape is also almost universal, especially when excommunication or actual death by stoning is threatened as a part of religious doctrine.

If we combine the Stockholm syndrome *(SS)* with another recognized psychological condition known as Cognitive Dissonance *(CD), we* have perfect storm for producing an uncompromising, unthinking religious convert. (6) Together they produce a victim who determinedly believes that their emotional, fairy tale attachment to the authority is not only acceptable but also needed for day-to-day survival. The acceptance of the unrealistic fairy tale allows the adult to utilize Cognitive Dissonance to rename fairy tales as true tales, even adding details, which may be partially true. Half-truths and distortions allow for a complete change their lifestyle to support beliefs that are obviously bizarre, by rational or logical standards.

Most people have a propensity to seek consistency in their beliefs and perceptions, even the extra sensory kind. What happens when one of our beliefs conflicts with recently discovered scientific evidence? This is where the term Cognitive Dissonance is used to describe the feeling of discomfort that results from holding two conflicting cognitions. When there is a discrepancy, something must change to reduce the dissonance. Cognitive Dissonance can occur in many areas of life, but it is particularly evident where an individual's behavior conflicts with beliefs that may be integral to his or her social or self-identity. Consider a situation in which a woman who obviously believes in and values her childhood beliefs in myths and fairy tales. As she matures she uncovers empirical evidence that exposes the believed-in fictions of childhood. As we intellectually mature, conflicts of this sort are exposed resulting in cognitive conflict.

To continue our example: First, it may be particularly important for her not to abandon the beliefs she personally devised as a growing child. Second, now she is reading, learning, and discovering evidence that contradicts her earlier beliefs.

In order to reduce the dissonance between earlier beliefs and recent evidence she can discard or reduce her emphasis on mythology by incorporating the modern evidence. Or she may rationalize the new evidence by verbalizing "its just another belief system". In the second option, dissonance is minimized by emphasizing the alleged mythical qualities of her childhood folklore rather than focusing on the obvious logical flaws in such reasoning.

There are three basic strategies to reduce cognitive dissonance:

- Focus on more supportive beliefs. Increase reading mythology and New Age literature, which in her mind outweigh the dissonant evidence.
- Reduce the importance of the conflicting belief. "Science is just another belief system."
- Change the conflicting belief. Put aside mythology and fairy tales so that newer thoughts are consistent with other recent empirical evidence and scientific discoveries.

Cognitive dissonance plays a role in many of our judgments, decisions, and evaluations. Becoming aware of how conflicting beliefs impact the decision-making process is a great way to improve any current ability to make faster and more accurate choices.

CD allows an individual to unconsciously modify information that produces uncomfortable feelings. When two sets of cognitions, data, empirical fact, knowledge, input from others, childhood beliefs, etc. are in opposition, the individual's emotional homeostasis becomes threatened and, thus, discomfort arises. Rather than admit the foolishness or the absurdity of a situation or irrational beliefs, some may attempt to reduce the dissonance. Often their mental perceptions and the attending rationales and cognitions do not make sense to objective observers. Only those who have held similar childhood fictions or have been indoctrinated by the same beliefs can agree. When a sympathetic group supports the same craziness it become even more firmly fixed.

A common example of cognitive dissonance occurs in the purchasing decisions we make on a regular basis. Most people want to hold the belief that they make good choices. When a product or item we purchase turns out badly, it conflicts with our previously existing belief about our decision-making abilities. In any case, Denial and Rationalization, two of the most popular ego-defense mechanisms may be employed to reduce the dissonance.

Other examples of Cognitive Dissonance can be found in cigarette smokers who are well aware of the health risks smoking entails. Thus they introduce Rationalization: "I've cut down to a half pack a day—approximately." "We all have to go someday..." "My father smoked until he was almost ninety." Or they employ

Denial: Smoking groups blame no smoking regulations as being unfair. Or the ever popular, "Scientific evidence is just another belief system."

Another common example comes from religion itself. "Only a few priests are pedophiles." The maturing believer, male or female, begins to see through the church mythology and illogic yet rationalizes that they receive comfort from other parts of Church or New Age rituals. "Besides all my best friends are still members." These are attempts to reduce Cognitive Dissonance.

Several studies suggest that when believers commit to activities that are difficult, uncomfortable, or even degrading, a deeper bonding will occur. For example: Women volunteer to wear burkas, initiation to Fraternities, growing up being terrorized by religious doctrines or myths, clitorectomy, (7) attendance at military schools. Almost any difficult ordeal creates a more intense bonding experience. By the time one reaches for rational alternatives, the person feels that they have invested so many emotions, cried so much, or become so vexed at the thought of changing systems, and/or are so intensely involved in their belief and in the relationships within their religion or support group, it must be seen through to the finish. When competing sets of cognitions are in opposition, the individual's emotional balance becomes susceptible and cognitive dissonance arises. Rather than admit the silliness, illogic or even the absurdity of their current situational beliefs, most will attempt to reduce the dissonance with Rationalization and/or

Denial. Occasionally, even mental aberration, or forms of psychosis, are incorporated as defense mechanisms.

It is important to recognize that both Stockholm syndrome and Cognitive Dissonance develop at an unconscious level. The believing victim does not intentionally invent this devoted attitude toward their indoctrinated belief system. Both SS and CD develop as a primal attempt to survive in controlling environments where, more often than not, the requirements of the church or support group creates disjointed and unresolved conflict, which only further increases the need for deeper commitment and bonding.

To clarify and answer the questions posed in this book, *Woman Aware,* it is incumbent on the reader to realize that the iceberg analogy is apt, as is the *Dragon in my garage* comparison. (8) Or as Shakespeare's Hamlet said, "There are more things in Heaven and Earth ... than are dreamed..." Perhaps it is time for the *Woman Aware* to awaken to the new empirical data available with a simple push of a button.

There are at least two major goals in making the *unconscious*—conscious. The first is allowing curiosity to morph into unbridled questing and questioning, which is a magnificent definition of spirituality. Questioning is how we may continually live with a sense of *awe* and *wonder.* The second goal is the questioning and challenging of ancient and/or modern authority. To question absurd, cognitively disparate beliefs held by so many sincere and eloquent cult leaders can be freeing to the unconscious. Within the Stockholm syndrome questioning is more difficult because those who hold their adherents enthralled with the energy of their charismatic intellect become dramatic heroes or even gods and goddesses.

CHAPTER 9

Whole is Greater than Sum of Parts

Synergism is defined as a dynamic state in which combined effort is favored over the effort of individual components. The eternal quest on the part of men and women to search for and find *the other* is how synergism seeks us out. Synergism also means that the combined effort cannot be predicted by knowing the efforts of the individual. For example, the term synergism also advocates that the male gender acting alone will not accomplish what could be accomplished in concert with the female gender, or visa versa. The birth of a child is a palpable example.

Why then, has humankind sought to install the singular individual component as the divine ideal? If we return to the singular worship of the God or the Goddess we find an obvious incompleteness in that it lacks synergistic power. It would seem that both males and females should ideally be able to emulate the divine. The installation of the male as the worshipful ideal deity seems strange in light of modern empirically derived facts.

The popular contemporary writers, Hanna Rosin, Liza Mundy and Sheryl Sandberg [1] have provided a plethora of documentation to confirm, once and for all, that the female gender is indeed equal or superior to the male. In light of these facts, we are left with several unanswered questions. In the United States and most other progressive nations it is widely acknowledged that women out-spend, out vote, out-educate and, of course, outlive males. Brute strength is still considered a male province, but other than the fashionable-with-the-masses gladiator sports and warfare, where else is it in demand these days? Why then are men still alleged to be the superior gender in most religious circles? Perhaps the answer may be found on the part of both men and women, and in their endeavor to create via opposition, competition and singularity rather than synergism.

IF the history of *Homo sapiens'* surplus of religions follows the same course as in centuries past, God and Goddess worship are fated to end, just as the worship of gods, goblins and gnomes have ended. As *Homo sapiens* evolve and continue their search toward *the other* and discover synergism and empirical-based answers, supernatural explanations carry less and less weight and will eventually fade. When empirical evidence pours in and myth and magic pour out of our educated mainstream, faith based beliefs lose credibility. In the near future the oppositional stance will fade and synergism will be seen as essential to emerging idealized veneration formulas.

Since more and more actuarial evidence is becoming available, the entire internet world is beginning to see, in real time, that those who boast about their Las Vegas winnings, or those who were just thinking about someone, when that someone called on the telephone, are also those who neglect to report their Las Vegas losses, or remember thoughts about that special someone when they didn't call. This not to say that such fuzzy mental viewpoints are not fun or that they have no ego massaging benefits; it simply means that as societies around the world become more literate and factual-information-based, synergism and empirical evidence will win the day. Correlations will cease being called manifestations. Galileo won. The earth is not the center of the universe, no matter how many believers with extra sensory perceptions, said or say otherwise. The Stockholm syndrome has been consensually verified enough times to validate observed empirical evidence and define it as scientific (2) rather than just another belief system. By the use of consensual scientific evidence, most logic would convince us that within the domain of human rationality and reason, a fire-breathing dragon does not reside in your garage no matter how often one's extra sensory perceptions or twisted neural synapses say it does. (3)

Something of a similar nature may be observed about the origin and development of certain popular religions. Where were the objective observers when the Quran, from which the Muslim religion was derived, was handed down to the Prophet Mohamed or the golden plates from which Latter Day Saint scriptures are taken, were presented to the Prophet Joseph Smith? Or the witnesses to the delivery of commandment engraved stone tablets to Moses? Apparently the prophet Mohamed, the prophet Smith, and Moses were the one and only recipients of selective God given words. Although the sacred scriptures they promoted include sections attributed to multiple authors, there's still only one guy as the missing-evidentiary bottleneck. Mohamed's scriptures were passed on verbally for many years, as were Smith's epiphanies. Has anyone else seen any factual, objective evidence? Did anyone take rubbings or make sketches of the deliveries? Has any empirical evidence shown up for any of the holy writings? Apparently followers are required to believe and accept by faith the extra sensory perceptions of Moses, St. Paul, Mohamed, Joseph Smith, and many others as well. Look closely and you'll see that most existing religions and cults have similar beginnings.

As human beings continue to progress intellectually, Old Religions or New Age cults that hinge on personalized *perceptual epiphanies,* will not stand up to today's growing requirement of objective rational scrutiny. This is especially true when the howl to have faith is a central demand and when supporters do nothing to establish verifiable credibility.

Once again a synergistic stance is necessary. A legitimate pursuit of the scientific method requires more than one assessment or observation.

As was suggested in *The Flexxible Brain,* (4) recent brain-scan science has time after time demonstrated that repetitive learning or training can physically change brain structures. Morphed, physically changed or *nodulized* brains, once indoctrinated, perceive only a singular point of view; the brain becomes fixated and unable to incorporate other data. When personalized extra-sensory perceptions become central and logic and rational thought no longer penetrate the newly developed brain *nodules* you can be sure that unconscious, indoctrination has occurred. When rites and ritualized meeting times are required and aided with physical movement or rhythmic chanting, human brain *nodule* growth responds with an exponential rate of fixation.

Recently there has been a worldwide recognition of emerging electronic technology as well as the resulting change in human brain structures. In fact, our current era has been called the decade of Internet and mobile device anecdotes. Electronic communicating has moved front and center in human brain development and exploration. New forms of interaction have become almost humdrum routines so that smart phones are now virtually hemorrhaging acronym witticisms and stirring video images. The transience of religious systems, like the hurricanes of America's east coast or the volatile Arab Spring, can no longer be contained within a single national, political or religious boundary. The news of these events reaches billions of people instantaneously.

Say what you will, and criticize if you must, but social media is here to stay and is doing the evidence-based educational work for the masses that clerics, ecclesiasts, and charismatic spiritual teachers were supposed to be doing. A teaching that still uses mythology and magic as a belief base is like a black hole, that sucks in and lobotomizes authentic spirituality based thought. This is a kind of event horizon**[6] and savvy young people all over the world are avoiding it. They are tapping their smart phones and doing the Twitter drill to pass on new information that is morphing and changing directions with each passing nano-second. Keeping up with such change requires new thought and new brain processes.

The old, rigid ways are being replaced; those who cling to mythology will be left behind like Galileo's science left the geo-centric believers behind. The masses are opining, debunking, and in general objecting to their current systems of theological governance. The desert religions, for example, represent anachronistic arenas in the Mid-east where live theater is being produced for the rest of the world to view in real time. This kind of current computerized media will quickly spot the living walking select that are now seen by a new generation as black holes that suck in, stone or behead female victims and then arrogantly spit them out in the name of their obsolete religious tradition. It is worth repeating: A religious creed that uses violence or the threat of violence to impose its beliefs is a black hole and to be avoided like an event horizon at all costs.

**[6] The inescapable boundary at the edge of a cosmic black hole

The synergistic model is beginning to incorporate the disenfranchised masses. The new world of young men and women immigrants who had been trained to remain separated from each other by their dualistic religions, even within their newly acquired cultures, now have a vocal medium that allows their synergistic voice to be heard. Today, around the globe the tens of millions on *Facebook* and *Twitter* are unflagging and strident in their promotion of synergism. Millions of intelligent kids, of both genders, are tapping and poking at their smart phones spelling out their desire for representative-based intelligent integration rather than the myth based custom of separation. It is little wonder that The Big Three religions are losing ground and governments are ordering the spying on or censorship of their own people.

In the minds of most Big Three religionists or New Age believers there is no problem with evidence that contradicts their extra-sensory visions or myth-driven belief systems. For them, the point-at-able empirical evidence pouring out of scientific laboratories is rationalized as merely another religion. When confronted with consensually valid and verifiable evidence that contradicts their belief systems, these believers declare that science is just another way of creating a faith driven religion. In the worldwide domain, technology and evidence driven science is on the rise impacting higher learning, while religion is losing ground. (5) One must wonder if "Science is just another religion," why is it not also diminishing?

Empirical scientific evidence may expect backlash from the old guard. Some faith driven activists must deny they have a problem with adherence to legend and mythology. They vociferously claim they have bigger, bonier, smellier fish to fry. Scientific influences, from every discipline while on the rise, are still said to be "not worth the time of day." This kind of claim creates Cognitive Dissonance and makes Rationalization and Denial defenses necessary to faith based believers.

In recent months the scientific evidence revealing the male gender's lack of superiority as well as the lack of female inferiority has brought about a new paradigm shift, based on the seeking and discovery of *the other,* in the context of synergism. This change allows for a model of amalgamation rather than separation. (6) The young participants in this new view no longer grumble about their status, their corporation titles, their children or the lack thereof. They enjoy an unequaled selection of life styles and employment opportunities. It appears that only the older generations of women are still grumbling about being on the short end of the gender stick. Traditional women's magazines are still crammed with various gripes but even while they are complaining, a new paradigm is taking hold. It appears that the older generation has yet to see through the articles appealing to mid-life crises or the not-so-subtle advertisements that peddle the ego-centered demand for gender based prerogatives and/or entitlements. Everything from face creams to tropical vacations are marketed with slick bytes: "Take time for yourself, you deserve the best!"

Woman Aware

The subliminal message to the older woman is: "You are still missing out."

Myrna Blyth, former editor of The Ladies Home Journal, has still another take. In her book *Spin Sisters*, Blyth says, "Narcissism is an advanced evolutionary stage of female liberation. Me, me, me means women can finally be free, free, free." Which in the minds of many younger persons is translated as the old divisive message meaning: "We women still play the aged, worn out gender game, which allows men to think they are in charge, while we do what we wish behind their backs."

The recent incorporation of synergism among young, modern, progressive women allows them to openly claim all the privileges customarily afforded chauvinistic men in bygone years. Additionally they have the mental and societal spending clout that has been newly minted by youthful synergistic thought. The obvious point is, young modern women in some more progressive areas can have a whole new array of bankable choices. They now have the opportunities previously reserved only for one or the other genders. In some progressive sub-cultures **IF** young women choose to stay home, have babies, clean house and have guys hop up and pull out their chairs when dining, that too can be among the available choices; their synergized male companions will oblige.

Today, the important question younger women may be asking: "Is it time for all of us to rethink our various roles and expectations? After all, if we women within this new paradigm of synergism want to seek employment, we can. If we don't, we won't! But perhaps we'd all be better off if we stopped inventing and then insisting on living by outmoded stereotypes or obsolete belief systems. Especially within the geography still controlled by The Big Three.

The emerging modus operandi in various modern democratic communities is: Be yourself, and do what enhances contentment for you. It seems so obvious that we will lack contentment in the ongoing religion based male/female dualistic system as long as we live our lives in the context of stereotypes and other people's expectations. (7) Most people understand that privileges given to women in times past were given as part of the special role women were expected to play, particularly in religion-dominated societies. The synergistic model melds the genders for a new kind of creative lifestyle. One and one no longer equals two because synergism is a dynamic state in which combined effort is greater than the effort of a single individual. As long as myth and magic are used as a surrogate for the synergistic relationship human evolution will be stymied. As long as *the other* is ignored as the essential half of the synergistic miracle *Homo sapiens* will be foiled in their attempt to advance.

CHAPTER 10

Awake

In the introduction to this book it was proposed that unconscious forces often keep us occupied in order to avoid thinking about some of the weighty topics of living, like death. Others have suggested that the major religions, e.g. The Big Three, incorporate various appeals to our human desire for continued life. That is, they say that if you choose the beliefs so very popular since the good old days, (1) their particular dogmas and rituals will facilitate the possible avoidance of death altogether. Most promise their believers eternal life in some paradise or other. They repeatedly suggest it is better to believe and hearken back to some idealized time, than to think about today. (2) However, written below is an appeal to a point of view of human death that, in my opinion, falls into the domain of today's here and now progressive thought.

"We are going to die, and that makes us the lucky ones. Most people are never going to die because they are never going to be born. The potential people who could have been here in my place but who will in fact never see the light of day outnumber the sand grains of

Arabia. Certainly those unborn ghosts include greater poets than Keats, scientists greater than Newton. We know this because the set of possible people allowed by our DNA so massively exceeds the set of actual people. In the teeth of these stupefying odds it is you and I, in our ordinariness, that are here."

-Richard Dawkins-

Rather than avoiding the topic of death by promising eternal life, Dr. Dawkins proposes that we not only recognize, but also celebrate the idea that today we are the lucky ones to have lived. Yes, we are part of the naturalistic process of life and death, of inhaling and exhaling, of yin and yang, of male and female. To have one without the other is to miss the miracle of synergism. We are of nature and from nature and we continue the journey of life in the full acknowledgement of nature's conventions and demands. Love is the mirror of nature and science is the poetry of nature.

Today the new American surface mantra is tolerance and acceptance of other points of view, no matter how they vary. That's our popular, newly minted PC point, isn't it? But why then do we still have prisons and mental institutions? Still, if a Politically Correct (PC) religious label is attached, certain groups can literally get away with murder. (3)

In contrast to this currently popular point of view of newly minted Politically Correct (PC) tolerance and coexistence, there really are certain eternal themes that pursue us through the eons of human lifetimes. Superstition is one and rational thought is another.

ACKNOWLEDGEMENTS

In the late 90s a book fell into my hands entitled *Unweaving the Rainbow.* I was visiting New Zealand at the time, and somehow connected the freshness of the ideas in the book with the bright, clean landscape all around. It was the first time I was truly aware of how an idea could make everything else connect with what was also so new, fresh and exciting in my head. That awareness led to the publication of *The True Believers* (2005) where I took a stab at contrasting "believing" and "thinking" and how once we have a "belief system" locked in, we tend to lock out "thinking" as a future course of action. For the next number of years Neuro science captured my imagination and as a result of that study, I published *(2011)* another book.

Next, the TED talks fixed my attention, particularly the presentations of some of the most remarkable and brilliant women I have ever had the privilege of hearing. Once again it was the intensity and freshness of the ideas presented by the women speakers that most impacted my thinking especially Sheryl Sandberg and Hanna Rosin. Talk about new, fresh and exciting! In America "times are not a changin'." Indeed, times have changed! A dear friend recently reminded me that today, in many other parts of the world, women like Angela

Merkel of Germany, Christine Fernandez of Argentina, Julia Gillard of Australia, and Helle Schmidt of Denmark continue to influence world politics with their fresh ideas.

My special gratitude must be extended to the bright, beautiful women of Palm Springs and Yosemite for their untiring support and help with this book: *Woman Awake*. My thanks and ceaseless appreciation to: Kay Huxford, Andree Kolling, Julie Elstner and a very special thank you to Anja Albosta, who painted this book's astonishing front cover.

NOTES

Introduction

1. www.rainn.org/statistics

2. See: WWW. Samharris.org "One of the most common objections to my position on free will is that accepting it could have terrible consequences, psychologically or socially. This is a strange rejoinder, analogous to what many religious people allege against atheism: Without a belief in God, human beings will cease to be good to one another. Both responses abandon any pretense of caring about what is true and merely changes the subject. But that does not mean we should never worry about the practical effects of holding specific beliefs. I can well imagine that some people might use the nonexistence of free will as a pretext for doing whatever they want, assuming that it's pointless to resist temptation or that there's no difference between good and evil. This is a misunderstanding of the situation, but I admit, a possible one. There is also the question of how we should raise children in light of what science tells us about the nature of the human mind."

3. See: Drunk Tank Pink 2013 by Sam Alter New York. Penguin

4. Obama Hope Poster Ref: Shepard Fairey http://www.huffingtonpost.com
The artist who created the iconic "**HOPE**" *poster*" Fairey pleaded guilty to copying the poster. Received two years probation.

5. **See: Hanna Rosin** www.theatlantic.com/hanna-rosin
   Hanna Rosin, an Atlantic national correspondent, is the author of the book *The End of Men* based on her story in the July/August 2010 Atlantic.

6. **Jay Fort REF:** *www.thegreatnesszone.com*
   Jay Forte, is a former financial executive and corporate educator, author and now business and motivational speaker.

CHAPTER ONE

MEN ASK

1. ***www.nytimes.com/interactive/2013/07/.../Women-in-the-Workplace.htm...***
   Jul 12, 2013—The number of private sector jobs held by **women** rose to a record level in June, surpassing the previous record set more than five years ago.

2. **SUPERIOR?**
   *www.goodreads.com/book/.../15779534-are-**women**-the-superior-gender.*
   Are **Women** the **Superior Gender**, has convincingly dealt with the topic of gender identity in a way that no other work has done before.

3. **Atkinson Kate** *Life after death* **A Novel**—One critic said: book was difficult to follow—she (the protagonist) died and came back to life so many times that after about 1/2 of the book I gave up. Another critical reader suggested: It was the kind of a book that I should have had a pencil and paper next to me while I read it so I could write down dates and names...Another critic said:— Ms. Atkinson's new novel, "Life After Life," soars above anything she's done or including David Mitchell's "Cloud Atlas" and Jim Crace's "Being Dead.

4. **New Age** is an umbrella term used to describe an organization of diverse groups that share an enthusiasm for the creation of a new era (or "New Age") exemplified by harmony and enlightenment. Even though there are no clear boundaries within the New Age community, several common themes unify the movement. The first is that the arrival of the New Age will initiate a heightened spiritual consciousness accompanied by social and personal transformation as demonstrated by the eradication of hunger, sickness, poverty, racism, sexism, and war. The second unifying theme is that individuals can get a foretaste of this enlightenment through personal spiritual transformation, healing, and growth. New Age ideas have many different origins from a variety of places, but most of them can be traced to Eastern religious traditions such as Hinduism, Buddhism, and other ancient religious traditions. New Age groups are often distinguished by their occult practices of psychic readings, Tarot cards, yoga, meditation strategies, and astrology. Many New Age groups also believe in various natural healing practices and traditional/alternative medicines including acupuncture, herbal therapy, natural foods, and spiritual healing. Even though there is no standard doctrine within the New Age Movement, many of their teachings focus on individual autonomy, relativism, and spiritualism.

5. **Naturalism**: a general understanding of reality and humanity's place within reality—Usually defined most briefly as the conclusion that the only reality is nature as gradually discovered by human intelligence using the tools of "experience" "reasoning" and "empirical evidence" in equal measure.

6. **Military training** (boot camp) had a positive effect… including decrease of neurotic tendency and had a significant negative effect on self-sufficiency and caused increase in isolation and decease in sociability.

    Ten years of continuous war, characterized by multiple deployments, elusive guerilla adversaries, and occupied civilian populations—seemingly more tilted toward resentment than <u>gratitude</u>—have taken a significant toll on US troops. In addition to those who have been killed, physically maimed, or neurologically impaired by combat, many U.S. soldiers have experienced debilitating psychological disorders including <u>post-traumatic stress disorder</u> (<u>PTSD</u>), <u>depression</u>, and anxiety. Large numbers are on antidepressants and other psychotropic medications, while the <u>suicide</u> rate among troops has risen to alarming levels. (Last year, the U.S. military saw more active duty soldiers <u>commit suicide</u> than die in combat—48 of them Marines.)

7. **Thomas Jefferson** (1743-1826) Third President of the U.S.A. Oversaw the Louisiana Purchase from France (1803), Sent the <u>Lewis and Clark Expedition</u> (1804–1806). Initiated a process of <u>Indian</u> tribal removal and relocation to the <u>Louisiana Territory</u> west of the <u>Mississippi River</u>, in order to open lands for eventual American settlers.

   While not a notable orator, Jefferson was a skilled writer and corresponded with many influential people in America and Europe throughout his adult life.

   Jefferson opposed slavery in his speeches and writing; but he took little political action to emancipate slaves, he owned hundreds of his own, and freed only a fraction of these in his life and will. *Jefferson* took, Sally *Hemings*, as his mistress, when she was in her teens and he was the 44-year-old American politician living in Paris **DNA analysis 1998 confirmed children** a number of unacknowledged children were his.

CHAPTER TWO

MEN

1. **Reasons for the great depression:**
   Stock Market Crash of 1929
   Many believe that the stock market crash that occurred on Black Tuesday, October 29, 1929 is one and the same with the

Great Depression. In fact, it was one of the major causes that led to the Great Depression.

Bank Failure Throughout the 30s, over 9,000 banks failed. Bank deposits were uninsured. As banks failed people lost their savings. Surviving banks, unsure of the economic situation and concerned for their own survival, stopped being willing to create new loans.

Reduction in Purchasing Across the Board

With the stock market crash and the fears of further economic woes, individuals from all classes stopped purchasing items. This then led to a reduction in the number of items produced and thus a reduction in the workforce. The unemployment rate also rose above 25%, which meant even less spending to help alleviate the economic situation.

American Economic Policy with Europe

As businesses began failing, the government created the Smoot-Hawley Tariff in 1930 to help protect American companies. This charged a high tax for imports thereby leading to less trade between America and foreign countries along with some economic retaliation.

Drought Conditions

While not a direct cause of the Great Depression, the drought that occurred in the Mississippi Valley in 1930 was of such proportions that many could not even pay their taxes or other debts and had to sell their farms for next to nothing.

2. **Rosie the Riveter**: Many people continue to interpret Rosie as a **feminist** icon, but revisionist historians stress that she was not. Different parties for similar reasons appropriated her: to beckon women into the workplace. Unfortunately for many women who had grown accustomed to working and the financial independence that resulted from their jobs, Rosie's purpose was extinguished at the end of the war. Although employers had grown to accept women in the workplace, the return of the soldiers to the home front forced them to admit that their recently adopted female staff had been only temporary—for the most part.

Those women who continued to work outside their homes were pressured to take more socially accepted and lower-paying jobs, like secretarial and vocational nursing positions. Although these gender disparities took hold once again, it was too late to close the floodgates. It wasn't long before the daughters of these American women began to chip away at archaic ideas, making way for the women of today to seek higher education and excel in professional roles. While the need for Rosie propaganda may no longer be necessary, her we-can-do-it attitude has left an imprint in history.

3. **Female longevity compared to male:** Although the reasons for women living longer than males may change with time and technology, it seems likely that women have been outliving men for centuries and perhaps longer. Men appear to have the deck stacked against them by biology. One way the cards are marked is that females have two X chromosomes, whereas males have an X and a Y—the latter being a runty little thing with only a small complement of genes. Females' "spare" X chromosome protects them from genetic mutations on the other one. Women are thus carriers of, but rarely suffer from, diseases like hemophilia, which are caused by the mutation of X-chromosome genes. A further biological difference between the sexes is in the lengths of their telomeres. These are sections of DNA that protect the ends of chromosomes from decay. Men's telomeres are shorter than those of women, and also degrade more quickly. The biggest biological difference between health of the sexes, however, can be summed up in a single word: testosterone. Testosterone is the hormone that more or less defines maleness (though women have it too, in lesser quantities). It promotes both aggression and risky behavior. It also suppresses the immune system, which is why castrated eunuchs live 13.5 years longer than men who are intact.

4. **King Abdullah:** The pace of reform in Saudi Arabia has reflected what seemed to be rationalization and denial. For years change has been almost imperceptibly slow. Recently, however, things have suddenly accelerated as the king has moved to show the ultraconservative Saudi religious establishment quite literally 'who's boss'. He sacked the head of the feared religious police and the minister of justice, appointed Nora al-Fayez as deputy

education minister, making her the highest-ranking female official in the country's history, and moved to equalize the education of women and men under the direction of a favored son-in-law who has been preparing for years to modernize the nation's school system. Abdullah waited biding his time until it was appropriate for him to make the changes he wanted. Whatever the reason, the 85-year-old monarch has begun acting like a leader whose vision is becoming clear just as time is running short. Last year King Abdullah opened a center for religious dialogue in Vienna that drew criticism because of Saudi Arabia's own lack of religious freedom. In 2008 he sponsored an interfaith conference in Spain. While in Saudi, women's freedoms are still severely limited. They are not allowed to drive but apparently private girls' schools are now allowed to hold sports activities in accordance with the rules of Sharia, or Islamic law. Students must adhere to "decent dress" codes and Saudi women teachers supervise the activities, according to the Education Ministry's requirements. The decision makes sports once again a stage for the push to improve women's rights, nearly a year after two Saudi female athletes made an unprecedented appearance at the Olympics.

CHAPTER THREE

PROTECTING

1. **Roula Yaacoub** was the 24th Lebanese woman to be killed in the past three years, and whose murder has thus far gone legally unpunished. She died from torture and abuse at the hands of her husband. Roula's murder, which took place in the town of Halba in northern Lebanon on July 9, has brought to the forefront the issue of the draft law on protecting women from domestic violence. After more than a year, the law made it to a parliamentary subcommittee tasked with studying it. The committee held its first meeting in May 2011, and that was enough to flare up the situation. As soon as the subcommittee launched

discussions, Muslim clerics impacted its members to the extent that the stances of some MPs seemed to be a reflection of what their religious authorities dictated.

Sunni clerics protest in opposition to the laws protecting women. During the protest, Sheikh Mohammed Bin Darwish Abu Qataa al-Naqshabandi delivered a speech calling for "dismissing the law from discussions, because it violates the sacredness of God and annuls "Islam—a religion that wishes to preserve the masculinity and manhood of the male, and every human being has rights."

Despite the deep political rift between Sunnis and Shiites in Lebanon, clerics from both sects agreed on the refusal of the draft law. E.g. "Whoever coerces his wife by violence and threat into sexual intercourse shall be imprisoned for offense of domestic violence." This article made both Sunnis and Shiites coordinate a movement rejecting women's protection. On July 26, 2011, the Sunni Mufti reiterated again, "Muslims in Lebanon refuse a draft law that violates the Sharia. Based on all these stances, it becomes clear that the reasons for their refusal are as follows:

First, the clerics refuse because their authority on personal status laws is undermined.

Second, the clerics refuse the principle of equality between men and women stipulated in secular Lebanese laws

Third, clerics refuse any clear and explicit secular law that punishes a man in the event that he physically abuses his wife or any woman that is seen as being under his control according to religious conviction. This is because according to some, this law negates the explicit aforementioned Quranic text (i.e., Surat An-Nisa', verse 34): "As to those women on whose part you fear disloyalty and ill-conduct, admonish them (first), (Next), refuse to share their beds, (And last) beat them (lightly); but if they return to obedience, seek not a way against them: For Allah is Most High, great (above you all)." A number of clerics see, in accordance with this verse, that beating a woman is possible and permitted.

Fourth, the clerics reject that marital rape be considered an offense. Suggesting laws on protecting women "introduces new crimes such as the heresy of the rape performed by the husband against his wife and the criminalization of this act."

Sheikh Nabil al-Wazza, "The obedience of the wife to the husband is an obligation in Islam." Sharia refuses to consider "the coercion of a wife into sexual intercourse as sexual assault; this is the right of the husband." Wazza averred, "Equality [between men and women] opposes the core of the Islamic faith."

Thus, after more than four years since the law was proposed, religious objections have succeeded in obstructing and preventing its approval. This is in addition to several other Lebanese laws making women victims of discrimination or ill treatment under the pretext of religious beliefs and laws of God that human beings are not entitled to modify or replace.

In the meantime, these crimes continue to claim the lives of women: 24 women were killed during the period of examination of the frozen draft law. Furthermore, 473 domestic violence-related complaints were lodged by women in 2009 in Mount Lebanon, while 353 other complaints—including cases of beatings, abuse and attempted murder—were also lodged. The judicial rulings issued by the Lebanese courts in 2010, in all domestic violence cases without exception, led to no condemnation of the aggressor and to the cessation of prosecution against him. This is because for some, religious norms and social traditions prevail over missing legal texts.

2. **Abuse of Muslim women** at the hands of their own husbands in North America is hidden and ignored by local communities. Domestic violence is the single major cause of injury to women in America. "Nearly one quarter of women in the United States—more than 12 million- will be abused by a current or former partner some time during their lives," according to the American Medical Association; and, despite Islamic teachings of "justice and compassion," many Muslim women in the United States and Canada are no exception to the statistic above. Based on information from Muslim leaders, social workers, and activists in North America, the North American Council for Muslim Women says that at least 10 percent of Muslim women are abused emotionally, physically, and sexually by their "devout"

Muslim husbands. (There are no hard numbers, because local community leaders haven't taken the well-known problem seriously enough to research.)

Despite the severity of the problem, the Muslim community has largely closed its eyes and devoted very few resources to helping the victims and stopping the abusers. This is doubly unfortunate because family violence is one of America's most critical health problems (according to the American Medical Association and the U.S. Surgeon General), and Islamic leadership is needed to deal with this crisis; but Muslims are clearly in no moral position to lead society because they commit and tolerate (Sharia laws appear to advocate) abuse within their own community.

In most Middle Eastern countries the Islamic value system has blocked the successful embrace of modern education—especially for women. This directly thwarts the creation of a middleclass that would be the driving force behind a future generalized economic transformation. This is clearly illustrated by the divergent paths taken by India and Pakistan. When compared, we see India has an educated and thriving middleclass, while Pakistan has not. Even though they were created from the same landmass in 1947, and share language, ethnicity and culinary habits, they are now truly divergent countries. Pakistan invested in Islam, not in modern education and as a result Pakistan has become a Sharia-shrine and a wellspring of jihad and terror. Pakistan's identification with Islam and the consequent emphasis on the Islamic doctrines acting as the "guiding force" is a clear explanation of why women remain abused and uneducated.

3. **A Muslim woman who became the disfigured face** of the shunned and forgotten women of Pakistan committed suicide, in Italy last week. Fakhra Yunus was only 22 when her husband of three years, Bilal Khar, a member of Pakistan's politically elite Khar family, threw acid on her face while she slept, Almost immediately after their marriage, Khar began abusing, and Yunus suffered at his hands for nearly three years before she ran away, according to reports. Khar soon located and attacked her in 2000, but he has not been arrested. Reporter Durrani (The Daily News) wrote of Yunus : "I have met many acid victims. Never

have I seen one as completely disfigured as Fakhra. She had not just become faceless; her body had also melted to the bone. Despite her stark and hopeless condition, the government of the Islamic Republic of Pakistan was not in the least God-fearing. She was provided nothing...but disdain...and trashed."

Acid attacks are prevalent in that attacks were at an all-time high in Pakistan, they are often the work of husbands who attack their wives as a form of revenge for refusing sexual advances or other proposals. More than 7,000 deliberate burning and the Progressive Women's Association of Pakistan in just two Pakistani towns between 1994 and 2008 recorded acid attacks against women. Basically, Muslim Sharia law protects the mall abusers and killers.

4. **Brainwashing:** Techniques used in totalitarian countries to bring people to submit. To effect a radical change in the ideas and beliefs of (a person), especially by methods based on isolation, sleeplessness, hunger, extreme discomfort, pain, and the alternation of kindness and cruelty. Actually the above is a favorite technique of abusive husbands.

   Indoctrination: the act of indoctrinating, or teaching or inculcating a doctrine, principle, or ideology, especially one with a specific point of view: e.g. religious indoctrination.

5. **Modern day stoning** Islamabad: A woman was stoned to death after a cell-phone was recovered from her possession in Pakistan. Her two cousins told a TV channel that Arifa Bibi was stoned to death by her uncle and relatives, the Daily Times reports. The relatives followed the orders of the panchayat (religions priest) in a village of Dera Ghazi Khan to stone the mother of two after she was found using a cell phone. Stoning remains the way Iranian women—are punished for committing adultery. The international group blasted a judicial council in Iraq, made up of 12 religious jurists, for inserting a stoning provision into a draft law where it had been previously removed.

   Last November, security agents with the country's judiciary moved the bodies of four women who had been stoned in Tehran, Iran. There are no statistics that indicate the number of stoning victims but human rights groups say Iranian authorities are holding at least 10 women who face execution by stoning on adultery charges, Human Rights Watch says.

6. Since 1947 the **Indian government has tried to provide incentives for girls'** school attendance through programs for midday meals, free books, and uniforms. This welfare thrust raised primary enrollment between 1951 and 1981. In 1986 the National Policy on Education decided to restructure education in tune with the social framework of each state, and with larger national goals. It emphasized that education was necessary for democracy, and central to the improvement of women's condition. The new policy aimed at social change through revised texts, curricula, increased funding for schools, expansion in the numbers of schools, and policy improvements. Emphasis was placed on expanding girls' occupational centre's and primary education; secondary and higher education; and rural and urban institutions. The report tried to connect problems like low school attendance with poverty, and the dependence on girls for housework and sibling day care. The National Literacy Mission also worked through female tutors in villages. Although the minimum marriage age is now eighteen for girls, many continue to be married much earlier. Therefore, at the secondary level, female dropout rates are high

7. When thinking about the **economic recession**, women exhibit less interest in alpha males in favor of guys who call themselves "natural followers," a new study suggests.

    The results are surprising because they fly in the face of what evolutionary psychologists expect from women's mate choices. According to evolutionary theory, women will seek men who provide resources and protection. The new study found that women do still prefer high earners for long-term partnerships and marriage, but that for the short term they seem less concerned about snagging a macho man during a recession.

    "Our findings tell us that external factors, such as an economic recession, may affect women's mate preferences," said study researcher Fay Julal, a psychologist at Southampton

Solent University in England. "What is interesting here is that we have shown that women's mate choices appear to shift during an economic recession."

Western men, particularly those with low education levels, will face a difficult road in the 21st century," write authors in The British Journal of Psychiatry. "It may be more difficult, on average, for men to adjust to a domestic role than for women to adjust to a work role."

A confluence of trends could change this ratio, they write, including fewer job options for men who no longer out-earn their partners. As the job options narrow, men begin to assume a more prominent role as caregivers in the home—a role traditionally associated with women. The recent economic downturn has been dubbed the "Mancession" for its disproportionate effect on traditional male industries, such as construction and manufacturing. Meanwhile, women are outpacing men in the pursuit of undergraduate and graduate degrees and becoming a larger share of primary household earners. Men's failure to fulfill the role of breadwinner is associated with greater male depression but if societal expectations are altered, men may experience less distress, write researchers Boadie Dunlop and Tanja Mletzko, both of Emory University School of Medicine. If men are innately less suited to care for young children and maintain households, then their increased contribution in this area could lead to lowered self-esteem and more depression. However, if women are better equipped to care for young children simply because they learn to be that way, through socialization, rather than because of biological differences between the sexes

8. *Fifty Shades of Grey* is a 2011 erotic romance novel by British author E. L. James. It traces the deepening relationship between a college graduate, Anastasia Steele, and a young business magnate, Christian Grey. It is notable for its explicitly erotic scenes featuring elements of sexual practices involving bondage/discipline, dominance/submission, and sadism/masochism (BDSM).

The second and third volumes, *Fifty Shades Darker* and *Fifty Shades Freed*, were published in 2012. *Fifty Shades of Grey* has topped best-seller lists around the world, including the United Kingdom and the United States. The series has sold over 70 million copies worldwide, with book rights having been sold in 37 countries, and set the record as the fastest-selling paperback of all time, surpassing the *Harry Potter* series.

9. If you can get past the studied jauntiness and occasionally histrionic style, Daniel Bergner's **What Do Women Want?** says some useful scientific things about female sexuality. It knits together anecdotal, case studies and scientific discovery to overturn some tenacious assumptions: that, unlike men, women aren't hardwired for promiscuity; that security and emotional connection are the most important factors in women's sexual transactions; that, above all, sexuality in women is constitutionally milder than in men. Or, as Bergner puts it: "That women's desire—its inherent range and innate power—is an underestimated and constrained force, even in our times. Rats are a big part of this book, as they often are in pop-science, which could boil down many of its arguments to "because a rat did it". Bergner spends time watching scientists watching rats for signs of what in humans might be considered inverse or atypical gender behavior.

Bergner finds case studies of women who feel guilty for not fancying the sweet, reliable men, opting instead for the unreliable risk-takers.

Bergner's point is that they titillate women by aligning more truly—which is to say neurologically—with their sexual impulses. Here is a woman with a nice fiancée, a guy who holds not only her hand, but her granny's hand, but who she doesn't want to have sex with because she's so busy fantasizing about her dashing and dangerous ex. The author extrapolates species-wide lessons from this, about female desire for male- **Fifty Shades** fantasy sex is compelling precisely because it is taboo, and therefore as much a social as an animal impulse.

The solid point is that women's sexuality is still bound up in strict ideas about evolution. As Helen O'Connell, an Australian urologist, puts it, "it boils down to the idea that one sex is sexual and the other is reproductive". Which is why, perhaps, overt sexuality in women over childbearing age is not considered attractive, while Robert Redford can still play a romantic lead.

The single strand of evolutionary psychology that argues women are inclined towards monogamy and "safe sex" for the protection of their children, while men, for equally good evolutionary reasons, are compelled to scatter their seed far and wide is suspect. Bergner writes, other studies undermine this completely, showing that in feral environments where male monkeys randomly kill babies in the group, a female monkey who has sex with as many males as possible obscures paternity of her child and stands a better chance of every male in the group protecting it. Or, in certain monkey societies, the female is dominant, a sexual aggressor who instigates sex and appears to want more of it than male monkeys. "Female rhesus monkeys run the sexual show, incite warfare, and rule their world.

The lives of modern women fare better, on the huge and growing problem of antidepressants; 15 million women in the US are on mood-stabilizing drugs, a common side effect of which is reduced sex drive. And Bergner is touching on the difficulty of sustaining interest in a partner over the course of a long marriage. It is enough, he writes, to make a sex therapist sigh.

One woman likens the pleasure of having sex with her husband to "the pleasure of returning library books".

10. Some still demand **special treatment**: most thinking people understand that **"privileges" given to women** in times past were given as part of the special "role" women were expected to play in society. Today in some of these stereotypical scenarios women are still placed on pedestals—often so high they restrict their activities—just as cinched-up corsets and hooped skirts did in other eras. But, on this, oft consensually agreed upon lofty perch, women are still looked-up-to and prized as adorable icons. Their alleged fragile sensibilities required men to refrain from certain behavior and language expletives in their presence. In the past, chivalry was a given, even to the point (as one legendary story suggests) of gallantly doffing a cloak and throwing it over a mud puddle to protect the feet of a thusly perched woman— albeit a queen. And today it seems that some modern feminist

women (e.g. MIT research biologist **Nancy Hopkins**) want similar deference while paradoxically insisting that men treat women as equivalent in labor and most social circumstances. The brouhaha she created cost Harvard president, **Larry Summers**, his job. As one NY Times reporter satirically wrote: "The foul brute may as well have rapped that women are "hos," or declared that they should be kept barefoot and pregnant. Nancy Hopkins' remarkable feminist exercise in self-parody, told reporters that she "felt I was going to be sick," that "my heart was pounding and my breath was shallow, and that she had to flee the room because otherwise "I would've either blacked out or thrown up." Such fatuous feminist fulminations may have been good fun in past eras, as have been the eviscerations of Hopkins as a latter-day "Victorian maiden exposed to male coarseness, [who] suffers the vapors and collapses on the drawing room carpet in a heap of crinolines." This may indeed be a case where a Divisive woman wants to have her 'cake and eat it too'.

CHAPTER 4

FLUNKING LESSONS

1. In 1985, *Ms.* Magazine conducted a national rape survey on college campuses in the United States, directed by Mary Koss, a professor of psychology at Kent State University. The survey asked 3,187 college women, selected at random nationwide, a series of ten questions related to **sexual violation**. Koss concluded that 15.4 percent of respondents had been raped, and that 12.1 percent had been victims of attempted rape.

    According to Christina Hoff Sommers, the oft-quoted "one in four" statistic is based upon flawed data. The criteria for the study was based on the question, "Have you had sexual intercourse when you didn't want to because a man gave you alcohol or drugs?" This, as professor Neil Gilbert pointed out, left the door open for anyone who regretted a sexual liaison to consider their partner a rapist.

In 1997, a National College Women Sexual Victimization (NCWSV) survey was conducted in the U.S. of 4,446 women, chosen randomly, who were attending a 2- or 4-year college or university during the previous semester. The survey consisted of behavioral-specific questions which describe an incident in graphic language and which covers the elements of a criminal offense, such as "Did someone make you have sexual intercourse by using force or threatening to harm you?" According to that survey, 1.7% of women had experienced a complete rape and another 1.1% had experienced an attempted rape. Campus rape at U.S. colleges has for years gone unchecked. A group of students taking legal action against six leading institutions may finally change that)

2. Of the 1,000 adults interviewed Dec. 17-18, the HuffPost/YouGov poll revealed 45 percent believe in **ghosts,** or that the **spirits** of dead people can come back in certain places and situations. When asked if they believe there's a life after death, 64 percent responded—Yes. While 59 percent of adults don't believe they've ever actually seen a ghost, 43 percent also don't think that ghosts or spirits can harm or interact with living people.

3. **Advanced education is highly correlated** with agnosticism rather than "faith". Professor Richard Lynn, emeritus professor of psychology at Ulster University, said many more members of the "intellectual elite" considered themselves atheists than the national average. A decline in religious observance over the last century was directly linked to a rise in average intelligence, he claimed.

Professor Lynn, who has provoked controversy in the past with research linking intelligence to race and sex, said university academics were less likely to believe in God than almost anyone else.

A survey of Royal Society fellows found that only 3.3 per cent believed in God—at a time when 68.5 per cent of the general UK population described themselves as believer. A separate poll in the 90s found only seven per cent of members of the American National Academy of Sciences believed in God.

Professor Lynn said most primary school children believed in God, but as they entered adolescence—and their (rational) intelligence increased—many started to have doubts. He told Times Higher Education magazine: "Why should fewer academics believe in God than the general population? I believe it is simply a matter of the IQ. Academics have higher IQs than the general population. Several Gallup poll studies of the general population have shown that those with higher IQs tend not to believe in God."

He said religious belief had declined across 137 developed nations in the 20th century at the same time as people became more intelligent.

4. **Deepak Chopra** (ref: Huffington post.com Deepak Chopra rescuing-**intelligent** design)

5. Meera Nanda's book ***Prophets Facing Backwards*** a critical look at the collision of Indian religion and science as well as the unwitting support of reactionary Hinduism by postmodern intellectuals in the West. Critique of Fundamentalist and Nationalist movements that abuse Postmodern theory to hijack science. She reminds us that scientific Modernism remains relevant in the face of reactionary movements like "Creation Science" in the West that continue to "face backwards" into an imaginary 'Dreamtime' while doing violence to their own scriptures that were never intended to be science lectures.

6. **Intuition** is the ability to acquire knowledge without inference and/or the use of reason "The word 'intuition' comes from the Latin word 'intueri' which is usually translated as 'to look inside' or 'to contemplate'." Intuition provides us with beliefs that we cannot justify in most cases. For this reason, it has been the subject of study in psychology, as well as a topic of interest for who believe in the **supernatural** The "right brain" is popularly associated with intuitive processes such as aesthetic abilities. Some scientists have contended that intuition is associated with innovation and epiphanies in scientific discovery. Intuition is also a common subject of New Age writings.

7. **Extending the "western science is evil" argument:** The underlying attitude is that the secularized, health and fitness oriented postural yoga is somehow now corrupted, inauthentic, fallen, tainted with Western decadence and devoid of psychological and spiritual meaning. Hindu purists seem incapable or unwilling to credit non Hindu Americans and other yoga practitioners with their own ability to integrate the postures they do with their own sense of spirituality. Thus they take on the role of a stern parent who has to teach a wayward child what his/her *real* interests, aims and beliefs ought to be—and all of them, invariably, turn out to be what the "5000 years old" tradition teaches! The old prejudice—or rather truthfully: chauvinism— "Hindu India" is described as the male guru of all nations and is what animates their ideologues.

CHAPTER 5

ACQUIESCENCE

1. **Evolve hotter.**
   A recent study revealed that women are getting better looking through evolution; meanwhile, men are staying the same. After following more than 2,000 people through four decades of life, the study showed that attractive women had 16 percent more children than average-looking chicks and that beautiful people are 36 percent more likely to have a daughter as their firstborn. All those gorgeous daughters mean more beautiful women than in past generations. See: Cosmo Magazine 1212

2. **Simone de Beauvior aka Simone-Lucie-Ernestine-Marie Bertrand de Beauvoir,** (French: [sim☐n də bovwa☐]; 9 January 1908 - 14 April 1986), was a French writer, intellectual, existentialist philosopher, political activist, feminist, and social theorist. While she did not consider herself a philosopher, Beauvoir had a significant influence on both feminist existentialism and feminist theory. She wrote novels, essays, biographies, an autobiography,

monographs on philosophy, politics, and social issues. She is best known for her novels, including *She Came to Stay* and *The Mandarins*, as well as her 1949 treatise *The Second Sex* Her analysis of contemporary feminism

3. **Sandberg** says her new best seller "***Lean In***" is about believing in ourselves and reaching for any ambition It's about each one of us asking ourselves what we would do if we weren't afraid and then reaching for those ambitions." She later reiterated to CNN reporter Kelly Wallace that, "the intention was for the message to be really inclusive." One woman, who attended and heard Sandberg's remarks, wrote that she believes Sandberg's message isn't elitist, or a "blame game." Rather it's "a call to action ... [for] women and men everywhere ... to realize all the ways in which we women unintentionally take a back seat at the conference room, instead of taking our due seat at the table, and the powerful cost of that reality.

Sheryl Sandberg has launched a powerful conversation about gender in the workplace, a topic that impacts *all* women. Hopefully more people will feel empowered to start talking about their own definitions of success—and what it takes to get it.

4. *Stereotype: Journal of Applied and Developmental Psychology 29, no1 (2008) 17-2camtriplehelix.com/journal/issue/17/allergic-to-algebra...of.../pdf

tests such as the SAT mathematical section. ... that when **women checked** the '**female**' gender **box ... the stereotype** threat was greatest. These findings show convincingly that stereotype threat significantly affects women's performance. These experiments strongly support the general assumption that it is the social stereotyping rather than any inherent biological traits, that accounts for the difference in male and female systemizing skills, and thus performance in mathematical exams or career choice. Ref: Begely S. The Math Gender Gap Explained. [homepage on the internet]. June 1, 2009 [cited 2012 Jul 4]. Available from: https://sites.google.com/ site/sbegley614/the-math-gender-gap-explained

5. Sandberg, Sheryl *Leaning in* (page 28) A.F Knoff NY 2013

6. Journal of Surgical Research 105 no (2000) 31-34

7. E. Gadon. *The Once and Future Goddess* Harper Collins 1989

8. **Literal interpretations of the Bible**: My "gay" neighbor wanted me to ask since so many "believers" follow the bible and condemn homosexuals. But what about the other "sacred texts?"
    1. Leviticus 25:44 states that I may possess slaves, both male and female, provided they are purchased from neighboring nations. A friend of mine claims that this applies to Mexicans, but not Canadians. Can you clarify? Why can't I own Canadians?
    2. I would like to sell my daughter into slavery, as sanctioned in Exodus 21:7. In this day and age, what do you think would be a fair price for her?
    3. I know that I am allowed no contact with a woman while she is in her period of menstrual uncleanness—Lev.15: 19-24. The problem is how do I tell? I have tried asking, but most women take offense.
    4. When I burn a bull on the altar as a sacrifice, I know it creates a pleasing odor for the Lord—Lev.1:9. The problem is, my neighbors. They claim the odor is not pleasing to them. Should I smite them?
    5. A neighbor insists on working on the Sabbath. Exodus 35:2. clearly states he should be put to death. Am I morally obligated to kill him myself, or should I ask the police to do it?
    6. A friend of mine feels that even though eating shellfish is an abomination—Lev. 11:10, it is a lesser abomination than homosexuality. I don't agree. Can you settle this? Are there 'degrees' of abomination?
    7. Lev. 21:20 states that I may not approach the altar of God if I have a defect in my sight. I have to admit that I wear reading glasses. Does my vision have to be 20/20, or is there some wiggle- room here?

8. Most of my male friends get their hair trimmed, including the hair around their temples, even though this is expressly forbidden by Lev. 19:27. How should they die?
9. I know from Lev. 11:6-8 that touching the skin of a dead pig makes me unclean, but may I still play football if I wear gloves?
10. My uncle has a farm. He violates Lev.19: 19 by planting two different crops in the same field, as does his wife by wearing garments made of two different kinds of thread (cotton/polyester blend). He also tends to curse and blaspheme a lot. Is it really necessary that we go to all the trouble of getting the whole town together to stone them? Lev.24:10-16.

Couldn't we just burn them to death at a private family affair, like we do with people who sleep with their in-laws? (Lev. 20:14)

I know "believers" have studied these things extensively and thus enjoy considerable expertise in such matters, so I am confident you can help. Thank you again for reminding us that God's word is eternal and unchanging.

9. **W. Dever** I am not reading the Bible as Scripture... I am in fact not even a theist. My view all along—and especially in the recent books—is first that the biblical narratives are indeed 'stories,' often fictional and almost always propagandistic, but that here and there they contain some valid historical information. That hardly makes me a 'maximalist. Archaeology as it is practiced today must be able to challenge, as well as confirm, the Bible stories. Some things described there really did happen, but others did not.

The Biblical narrative about Abraham, Moses, Joshua and Solomon probably reflect some historical memories of people and places, but the 'larger than life' portraits of the Bible are unrealistic and contradicted by the archaeological evidence. Ref: Dever, William "The Contribution of Archeology to the study of Canaanite and Early Israelite Religion." *Ancient Israelite Religion. Philadelphia. Fortress Press. 1987.*

CHAPTER 6

THE HEBREW CHRONICLES

1. Sanders, *The Epic of Gilgamesh,* This epic poem is the oldest known to exist in history, predating Hebrew literature by at least 1000 years. Gilgamesh, the hero, discovers he has godly blood, so sets out on a journey to the land of the gods in an attempt to gain entry. It is of ancient Sumerian origin, from the land called Mesopotamia. It is an important work for those studying ancient literature, history and mythology. This Babylonian version is one of the oldest known, if not the oldest. Later renditions are more common and seem to embellish the story, so this work is important for serious researchers.

2. **William Dever:** From the beginnings of what we call biblical archeology, perhaps 150 years ago, scholars, mostly western scholars, have attempted to use archeological data to prove the Bible. And for a long time it was thought to work. [William Foxwell] Albright, the great father of our discipline, often spoke of the "archeological revolution." Well, the revolution has come but not in the way that Albright thought. The truth of the matter today is that archeology raises more questions about the historical accuracy of the Hebrew Bible and even the New Testament than it provides answers. That's very disturbing to some people. I have always thought that if we resurrected someone from the past, one of the biblical writers, they would be amused. I think they would have said, faith is faith is faith—take your proofs and go ...The fact is—archeology can never prove any theological suppositions of the Bible.

    "In other words, what did the biblical writers think they were doing? Writing objective history? No. That's a modern discipline. They were telling stories. The Bible is didactic literature; it wants to teach, not to describe. We try to make the Bible something it is not, and that's doing an injustice to the biblical writers. They were good storytellers." Dever, William G. (March/April 2006). "The Western Cultural Tradition Is at Risk". *Biblical Archaeology Review* 32 (2): 26 & 76.

See also: <u>Thomas L. Thompson's</u> *<u>The Historicity of the Patriarchal Narratives</u>* (1974), and <u>John Van Seters'</u> *<u>Abraham in History and Tradition</u>* (1975).

3. **See:** Gadon *the once and future goddess*—page 168) **Gadon's book *Once and future goddess*** has a cultural anthropology point of view. It describes and documents, with words and a good amount of black and white as well as several color photos, the 30,000 yr reign of the Goddess and her consort, and Her many forms throughout all of humanity—until Her people's agricultural lifestyle was destroyed by warrior societies looking for more to conquer and add to their wealth. "The Once & Future Goddess" tells the story of how women came to be oppressed in just the last 3,000 to 4,000 years by the dogma of the nomadic Jewish tribes, the political control of the Romans, and the re-interpretation of the teaching of the man commonly called Jesus by his disciple Paul, leading to the creation of Christianity and Judaism as well as Islam All three of "The Big Three" calling the first woman a sinner and traitor. Gadon's book gives women, the sense that history is also her story ... 30,000 years of archaeological evidence doesn't lie! Women were not perceived as evil or disgusting in any way, and were treated as equal or superior to men. The women of the Fertile Crescent area created fine art, mathematics, weavings, food, agriculture, theatre, music, and more, all the while sustaining a generally peaceful lifestyle with their neighbors.

4. **See** Film *The Graduate*' 1967 by Mike Nichols

5. As it turns out, the well-known Jewish commentator and author, Rabbi David Wolpe also knew about the Exodus fiction. In his article titled, "**<u>Did the Exodus Really Happen?</u>**" he mentions how other Rabbis wanted him to keep the fact that the Exodus story isn't true on the 'down-low'. The basic story of the Exodus from Egypt was touted as one of the most historical aspects of the <u>Bible</u> and yet it never happened. Further, how immoral is it for modern Jews to continue this myth at the expense of Egyptian dignity? For thousands of years the Jews have

blamed the Egyptians for enslaving their ancestors when that never actually happened. By continuing to celebrate Passover without acknowledging the truth of history only perpetuates the shame. They need to acknowledge that the celebration is based on a fictional story and that the Egyptians never enslaved the Jews.

6. **See references:** Old Testament Bible—Genesis and Exodus

7. **Merneptah victory stele:** (c.1209/1208 BC), begins with a laudatory recital of Merneptah's achievements in battle. The stele has gained much notoriety and fame for being the only Egyptian document generally accepted as mentioning "Isrir" or "Israel". It is also, by far, the earliest known attestation of Israel. For this reason, many scholars refer to it as the "Israel stele". This title is somewhat misleading because the stele is clearly not concerned about Israel—it mentions Israel only in passing. There is only one line about Israel—"Israel is wasted, bare of seed" or "Israel lies waste, its seed no longer exists"—and very little about the region of Canaan. Israel is simply grouped together with three other defeated states in Canaan (Gezer, Yanoam and Ashkelon) in the stele. Merneptah inserts just a single stanza to the Canaanite campaigns but multiple stanzas to his defeat of the Libyans.

8. The oldest surviving **bio of Mohamed**. (833CE) Ibn Hisham tells that before the revelation of the Qur'an, Mohamed would retreat for month every year to HIRA in Mecca. One year the prophet retreated from HIRA I the month of Ramadhan when he was visited by the angel Gabriel ... who presented him with several virses of the Quran According to Ibn Hisham, Gabriel appeared to Muhammad in his sleep, carrying a book. He commanded him to "read." Muhammad refused the order twice before finally asking what he was supposed to read. Gabriel replied with verses of the Qur'an.

9. **I Cor 14:34-35** Women should remain silent in the churches. They are not allowed to speak, but must be in submission, as the law says. If they want to inquire about something, they should ask

their own husbands at home; for it is disgraceful for a woman to speak in the church.

I Tim 2:12-15 "Now I permit a woman neither to teach nor exercise authority over a man, but let her be in quietness. For Adam was first formed, then Eve. And Adam was not deceived [when he sinned]; but the woman, having [first] been thoroughly deceived, became [involved] in the transgression [of Adam], and she will be saved by the Child-bearing [i.e., the bearing of Jesus Christ], if they abide in faith, and love and sanctification with self-restraint.

10. **Persecution vs Prosecution:** Candida Moss, a professor of Christianity at the University of Notre Dame and a Catholic, wants to shatter what she calls the "myth" of martyrdom in the Christian faith. Sunday school tales of early Christians being rounded up at their secret catacomb meetings and thrown to the lions by evil Romans are mere fairy tales, Moss writes in a new book. In fact, in the first 250 years of Christianity, Romans mostly regarded the religion's practitioners as meddlesome members of a superstitious cult. The government actively persecuted Christians for only about 10 years, Moss suggests, and even then intermittently. And, she says, many of the best-known early stories of brave Christian martyrs were entirely fabricated. The controversial thesis, laid out in *"The Myth of Persecution: How Early Christians Invented a Story of Martyrdom,"* has earned her a lot of hate mail and a few sidelong looks from fellow faculty members. But Moss maintains that the Roman Catholic Church and historians have known for centuries that most early Christian martyr stories were exaggerated or invented.

A small group of priest scholars in the 17th century began sifting through the myths, discrediting not only embellished stories about saints (including that St. George slew a dragon) but also tossing out popular stories about early Christian martyrs. Historians, including Moss, say only a handful of martyrdom stories from the first 300 years of Christianity—which includes the reign of the cruel, Christian-loathing Nero—are verifiable. (Saint Perpetua of Carthage, pictured in the stained glass window above, is one of the six famous early Christian martyrs Moss believes was actually killed for her faith.)Moss contends that when Christians were executed, it was often not because of their religious beliefs but because they wouldn't follow Roman rules. Many laws that led to early Christians' execution were not specifically targeted at them—such as a law requiring all Roman citizens to engage in a public sacrifice to the gods—but their refusal to observe those laws and other mores of Roman society led to their deaths. Moss calls early Christians "rude, subversive and disrespectful," noting that they refused to swear oaths, join the military or participate in any other part of Roman society.

Moss can at times seem clinical when attempting to distinguish between true and systematic persecution. "If persecution is to be defined as hostility toward a group because of its religious beliefs, then surely it is important that the Romans intended to target Christians," she writes. "Otherwise this is prosecution, not persecution. "With true government persecution, victims have no room to negotiate when trying to convince the government to stop targeting them, Moss said. But when the government's laws inadvertently lead to the persecution of Christians, there remains room for dialogue and debate over changing those laws.

"The reason I make the distinction is in the case of people seeking you out, torturing you just because you're Christian—which did happen for a few years—in that situation, you can't negotiate," she said. "You have no opportunity to resist or to fight back. In a situation where there's an assortment of disagreements ... there's room for dialog

11. **Skepticism** regarding these particular scriptural writings was partly occasioned by the rather extreme praise of celibacy found often associated with certain Gnostic groups. It is certainly possible that the present form of the text reflects the preferences or even the insertions of Gnostic editors; it is also possible that Orthodox editors toned down the text, which was then even more extreme. Tertullian, ca 190) spoke against these texts primarily for their advocacy of women as able to preach or baptize. Despite such disapproval, many versions—Latin, Coptic, Greek, and

Ethiopic—have survived, indicating that it circulated widely and was used over many centuries. In any case, the text appears to follow the form of ACTs in that the life of St. Thecla followed the course of her acts. Whether every word attributed to St. Paul was accurately recorded is not known. The physical description of Paul in 1:7 is very famous, and in agreement with iconographic depictions.

CHAPTER 7

UNCONSCIOUS INFLUENCE

1. **Schelling**—Friedrich Wilhelm Joseph von Schelling (1775–1854) is, along with J.G. Fichte and G.W.F. Hegel, one of the three most influential thinkers in the tradition of 'German Idealism'. Although he is often regarded as a philosophical Proteus who changed his conception so radically and so often that it is hard to attribute one clear philosophical conception to him, Schelling was in fact often an impressively rigorous logical thinker. In the era during which Schelling was writing, so much was changing in philosophy that a stable, fixed point of view was as likely to lead to a failure to grasp important new developments as it was to lead to a defensible philosophical system. Schelling's continuing importance today relates mainly to three aspects of his work. The first is his *Naturphilosophie*, which opens the possibility of a modern hermeneutic view of nature that does not restrict nature's significance to what can be established about it in scientific terms. The second is his anti-Cartesian account of subjectivity, which prefigures some of the best ideas of thinkers like Nietzsche, Heidegger, and Jacques Lacan, in showing how the thinking subject cannot be fully transparent to itself. The third is his later critique of Hegelian Idealism, which influenced Kierkegaard, Marx, Nietzsche, Heidegger,

2. Kate Becker on February 18, 2012 5:45 **KIDS NOVA** PM |http://www.pbs.org/wgbh/nova/insidenova/2012/02/early-experiences.html—thread

3. **Judith Harris** *The Nurture Assumption* *The Nurture Assumption* was first published a decade ago. In it, Harris argues it's not what parents do or say that determines who their children become—what really matters is the influence of peers... With parents seeming to worry more than ever about what it takes to raising a smart, decent kid, Harris's message may even sound reassuring. TIME Magazine's Kathleen Kingsbury caught up with Harris and asked:

   How strongly do you believe *The Nurture Assumption's* assertions hold up? Ans: "They've held up quite well. I took an extreme position: that parents have no important long-term effects on their children's personalities. One traditional developmental [psychologist] even admitted, not long ago, that they still can't prove that parents have any long-term effects on children."

   You distinguish between moral attitudes and personality traits in terms of the extent each are molded by influences outside the home. What sets them apart? "It hinges on the distinction between socialization and personality development. The strongest influence on morality is the local culture or subculture. But this influence may be different in different situations. For example, according to the local culture, it might be okay to cheat on a test in school but not okay to cheat in sports. Socialization adapts children to their culture—they learn to behave in the manner approved by their culture."

   Personality development, on the other hand, is not about conformity. Differences in personality don't go away during childhood and adolescence—they may even widen.

4. **Harlow, Harry:** Somehow, the conditions of deprivation change the brains and bodies of young children. At the Yerkes National Primate Research Center, <u>Mark Sanchez</u> is studying the question of *how* with Harlow's old subjects—rhesus monkeys. But these monkeys are not caged and separated from their mothers. It turns out that between two and five percent of female monkeys are naturally "bad mothers"—they abuse their babies, dragging them screaming across the ground, or they simply ignore them when they seek attention and comfort. These abused and rejected

infants spend more time screaming and throwing tantrums than warmly-mothered monkeys; they respond anxiously to new or stressful situations. And, their levels of the stress hormone *cortisol* are chronically high.

Not all monkeys respond equally—"genetic vulnerabilities" (or sensitivities, if you like) seem to amplify the damaging effects of abuse and rejection. Contrary to what might be expected, rejection is actually more destructive than abuse: Rejection was linked to low levels of serotonin in the brain and was the strongest predictor of whether a monkey would perpetuate the cycle of bad mothering in the next generation.

5. Dawkins: http://www.examiner.com/article/richard-dawkins-religious-indoctrination-is-child-abuse. For example, "how could children in religious education classes fail to be inspired if we could get across to them some inkling of the age of the universe? Suppose that, at the moment of Christ's death, the news of it had started traveling at the maximum possible speed around the universe outwards from the earth. How far would the terrible tidings have traveled by now? Following the theory of special relativity, the answer is that the news could not, under any circumstances whatever, have reached more that one-fiftieth of the way across one galaxy—not one- thousandth of the way to our nearest neighboring galaxy in the 100-million-galaxy-strong universe. The universe at large couldn't possibly be anything other than indifferent to Christ, his birth, his passion, and his death. Even such momentous news as the origin of life on Earth could have traveled only across our little local cluster of galaxies. Yet so ancient was that event on our earthly time-scale that, if you span its age with your open arms, the whole of human history, the whole of human culture, would fall in the dust from your fingertip at a single stroke of a nail file.

The argument from design, an important part of the history of religion, wouldn't be ignored in my religious education classes, needless to say. The children would look at the spellbinding wonders of the living kingdoms and would consider Darwinism alongside the creationist alternatives and make up their own minds. I think the children would have no difficulty in making up their minds if presented with the evidence.

It would also be interesting to teach more than one theory of creation. The dominant one in this culture happens to be the Jewish creation myth, which is taken over from the Babylonian creation myth. There are, of course, lots and lots of others, and perhaps they should all be given equal time. I understand that there are Hindus who believe that the world was created in a cosmic butter churn and Nigerian peoples who believe that the world was created by God from the excrement of ants...

Biblical or Delphic prophecies don't begin to aspire to such accuracy; astrologers and Nostradamians dare not commit themselves to factual prognostications but, rather, disguise their charlatanry in a vagueness smokescreen. When comets have appeared in the past, they've often been taken as portents of disaster. Astrology has played an important part in various religious traditions, including Hinduism. Notwithstanding astrology predictions—Halley'sl Comet will return without fail in the year 2062—you can take that to the bank."

Still another level of child abuse may be gleaned from the following: WHAT IS THE BEST **WAY TO STOP A CHILD** FROM BECOMING A SELF STARTING THINKER?

Never expose them to critical thinking, logic or empirical science.

Plus: Teach them the myths about how the world works and feed them with a steady died of mumbo jumbo dressed up like real knowledge.

Convince them that they are worthless and in need of redemption. Tell them that everything about their bodies that is enjoyable is grievously wrong to even think about. (Particularly thoughts about he opposite sex)

Instruct them with all severity that they should never question authority and be sure they are taught the difference between religious truth and error—between what one raving lunatic in the desert said about a jealous, vicious god who killed people because they were "not his chosen people" and another desert lunatic who demanded that his followers kill the "infidel non-believers".

Above all, be sure they "believe" rather than "think". Be sure they know that higher education is a waste of time and that they should learn to read at an eighth grade level and only read "spiritual" material.

That should do it

6. **See *Drunk Tank Pink* and other unexpected forces that shape how we think, feel and behave. Penguin Press, New York 2012**

7. *Darwin's Dangerous Idea: Evolution and the Meanings of Life* (1995) is a book by Daniel Dennett which looks at some of the repercussions of Darwinian theory. The crux of the argument is that whether or not Darwin's theories are overturned there is no going back from the dangerous idea that design—purpose or what something is for—might not need a designer. Dennett makes this claim because he thinks that natural selection is a blind process, which is nevertheless sufficiently powerful to explain the evolution of life. Darwin's discovery was that the generation of life worked algorithmically, that processes behind it work in such a way that given these processes the results that they tend toward must be so. Dennett thinks, for example, that by claiming that minds cannot be reduced to purely algorithmic processes, many of his eminent contemporaries are claiming that miracles can occur. These assertions have generated a great deal of debate and discussion in the general public. The book was a finalist for the 1995 National Book Award in non-fiction and the 1996 Pulitzer Prize for general non-fiction.

8. **Science : Educational Psychology News** Stanford University
http://neurosciencenews.com/neuropsychology-stress-learning-mineralocorticoid-receptors-350/

CHAPTER 8

THE CONSCIOUS WOMAN

1. **Harpers:** RICHARD RODRIQUEZ—From the July 2013 issue READINGS—From the July 2013 issue.

2. New York Times
   Published 4:00 am, Tuesday, January 16, 2007
   For what experts say is probably the first time, more American women are living without a husband than with one, according to a New York Times analysis of **census results**.
   In 2005, 51 percent of women said they were living without a spouse, up from 35 percent in 1950 and 49 percent in 2000.
   Coupled with the fact that in 2005, married couples became a minority of all American households for the first time, the trend could ultimately shape a range of social and workplace policies, including the ways government and employers distribute benefits.

3. **http://unstats.un.org/unsd/demographic/products/indwm/**

4. The **Stockholm syndrome** explains what happens in hostage-taking situations, but can also be used to understand the behavior of battered spouses, members of religious cults, Holocaust victims, household pets, and perhaps even users of Internet. I think it may also help explain the popularity of some governments as well as adherents to revelation type religions.

5. **Steven Weinberg** : American theoretical physicist and Nobel laureate in Physics for his contributions with Abdus Salam and Sheldon Glashow to the unification of the weak force and electromagnetic interaction between elementary particles.
   He holds the Josey Regental Chair in Science at the University of Texas at Austin, where he is a member of the Physics and Astronomy Departments. His research on elementary particles and cosmology has been honored with numerous prizes and awards, including in 1979 the Nobel Prize in Physics and in

1991 the National Medal of Science. In 2004 he received the Benjamin Franklin Medal of the American Philosophical Society, with a citation that said he is "considered by many to be the preeminent theoretical physicist alive in the world today." He has been elected to the U.S. National Academy of Sciences and Britain's Royal Society, as well as to the American Philosophical Society and the American Academy of Arts and Sciences.

Articles of his on various subjects appear from time to time in The New York Review of Books and other periodicals.

6. Leon Festinger first coined the term "**Cognitive Dissonance**". He had observed a cult (1956) in which members gave up their homes, incomes, and jobs. This cult believed in messages from outer space that predicted the day the world would end by a flood. As firm believers, they believed they would be saved by flying saucers at an appointed time. As they waited to be taken by flying saucers at the specified time, the end-of-the-world came and went. No flood and no flying saucer! Rather than believing they were foolish after all that personal and emotional investment—they decided their beliefs had actually saved the world from the flood and they became firmer in their beliefs after the failure of the prophecy. The moral: the more you invest (income, job, home, time, effort, etc.) the stronger your need to justify your position.

See: The Stockholm Syndrome and Cognitive Dissonance

7. **Islam is a non-negotiable coda**.

"Circumcision is obligatory (O: for both men and women). For men it consists of removing the prepuce from the penis, and for women, removing the prepuce (Ar. Bazr) of the clitoris."—Page 59, *Umdat al-Salik* ("Reliance of the Traveler"), a manual of Islamic jurisprudence certified as "reliable" by Egypt's very own Al-Azhar University

We **successfully beat back and defeated** a **sharia-compliant proposal** by the American Academy of Pediatrics to change a longstanding policy concerning the practice of clitorectomies in Islamic culture. The American Academy of

Pediatrics suggested that American doctors be given permission to perform a "ceremonial nick" on girls from Islamic countries

Well, you know.... when they do this, the female DRIVES are still intact because they don't remove the ovaries or uterus. It's just that the nerves and organs necessary to adult sexuality are removed and destroyed. The desire is there, but no way to find peace. LOTS of frustrated, bitter, unfulfilled women out for revenge... is this 'Why' they perpetrate it on their daughters?

8. **Ice berg analogy:** Used to illustrate Freud's structure of the human mind. The mind is likened to an iceberg, only the tip of an iceberg, or the mind, is visible. This is our conscious, or awareness. Just under the water line is our preconscious or dream state. The vast bulk of the iceberg or mind is hidden from view. We are unaware of it. This is our unconscious. Our unconscious contains our instincts, passions and fears. It is where long-forgotten memories of personality-forming experiences are held. Often parts of an iceberg break off and float to the surface. Likewise Freud thought bits of our unconscious could break off, and float to the surface of our conscious awareness in terms of neuroses. "Iceberg Analogy" Google lists over 73,500 results

8b **Dragon in garage**

A story of comparison for those who live by faith in something:

"A fire-breathing dragon lives in my garage"

Surely you'd want to check it out, see for yourself. There have been innumerable stories of dragons over the centuries, but no real evidence. What an opportunity!

"Show me," you say. I lead you to my garage. You look inside and see a ladder, empty paint cans, an old tricycle—but no dragon.

"Where's the dragon?" you ask.

"Oh, she's right here," I reply, waving vaguely. "I neglected to mention that she's an invisible dragon but I have special senses with which to "perceive her."

You propose spreading flour on the floor of the garage to capture the dragon's footprints. "Good idea," I say, "but this dragon floats in the air. "Then you'll use an infrared sensor to detect the invisible fire.

"Good idea, but the invisible fire is also heatless."

You'll spray-paint the dragon and make her visible.

"Good idea, but she's an incorporeal dragon and the paint won't stick." And so on. I counter every physical test you propose with a special explanation of why it won't work.

Now, what's the difference between an invisible, incorporeal, floating dragon who spits heatless fire and no dragon at all? If there's no way to disprove my contention, no conceivable experiment that would count against it, what does it mean to say that the dragon exists? The only thing you've really learned from my insistence that there's a dragon in my garage is that something funny is going on <u>inside my</u> <u>head</u>. You'd wonder if no physical tests apply, what convinced me. The possibility that it was a dream or a hallucination would certainly enter your mind. But then, why am I taking it so seriously? Maybe I need help. But maybe all those ancient European and Chinese myths about dragons weren't myths at all. Gratifyingly, some dragon-size footprints in the flour are now reported. But they're never made when a skeptic is looking. An alternative explanation presents itself. On close examination it seems clear that the footprints could have been faked. Another dragon enthusiast shows up with a burnt finger and attributes it to a rare physical manifestation of the dragon's fiery breath. But again, other possibilities exist. We understand that there are other ways to burn fingers besides the breath of invisible dragons. Such "evidence"—no matter how important the dragon advocates consider it—is far from compelling. Once again, the only sensible approach is to reject the dragon hypothesis and to wonder what the cause might be that many apparently sane and sober people believe in invisible dragons.

CHAPTER 9

SYNERGISM AND GENDER

1. **Hanna Rosen, Liz Mundy, and Cheryl Sandberg** have written best sellers about the condition of women in today's world.

2. **Is science just another religion? It just comes down to believing & having faith doesn't it?** The short answer is NO. Science is based on repeatable, verifiable evidence. Intuition is a good beginning and when its' epiphany is verified by repeatedly following the scientific method then it too moves into the realm of science—but perhaps only temporality—since one of the hallmarks of science is to keep questioning the data as new data appears…(unlike mythic and magic believing religions, who typically stay fixed in their revealed truths) Christian 'creationists' often make the same claim (ie science is a religion) then continue down the "6 day creation myth" as if it were evidence simply because it has endured. The fact of evolution is overwhelming—the evidence from so many varied disciplines, all of whom, on a daily basis produce new evidence in support of Darwin's basic contention. They question, examine, find evidence and only then do they agree to support evolution. The evidence from these various disciplines is freely available without interpretation from some 'epiphanized guru'.

It appears that Human beings have a natural proclivity to seek explanations and/or answers. Obviously we long to understand our vast mysterious universe. I suspect it is the reason so many and varied cults exist—in various ways, they aspire to provide explanations. Without a charismatic "leader" alleging to have "discovered" cosmic answers or a unique theory of an available "afterlife," few would endure.

Science tells us that the universe is expanding and like a great cosmic breath may contract again—maybe not. Some speculate that there are many universes, perhaps with Darwinian "selection" among the various universes. Perhaps not—Who knows? We can speculate and that can be fun but when mythical speculation becomes concretized in the brains of sycophant devotees the result can be mind numbing for them. Cognitive Dissonance occurs and rationalization and denial of a non-sense origin are usually the winners.

Is there a need for zealotry in exposing mind-numbing mythology? I think there is a need for confrontation of popular, intellect damaging, fashionable (common) beliefs. (eg see Muslim school records) There is an important difference about feeling strongly about something that I have examined and found evidence for—and feeling strongly about something because it has been "revealed."

3. "A fire-breathing dragon lives in my garage" See note 8 (b) in chapter 8

    Surely you'd want to check it out, see for yourself. There have been innumerable stories of dragons over the centuries, but no real evidence. What an opportunity for a "believer"!

    "Show me," you say.

4. Milton Robert. *2011The* **Flexxible** *Brain & Neuronastics Authorhouse* Bloomington IN

5. **religion losing ground http://www.huffingtonpost.com/ john-shook-phd/churchgoers-now-a-minorit_b_1537108. html**

6. *The Richer Sex* 2012 Simon and Shuster.
   The End of Men 2012 Penguin group

7. Most thinking people understand that "privileges" given to women in times past were given as part of the special "**role**" **women were expected to play** in society. Today some of these stereotypical scenarios women still place women on pedestals—often so high they restrict their activities just as cinched-up corsets and hooped skirts did in other eras. But, on this, oft consensually agreed upon lofty perch, women are still looked-up-to and prized as adorable icons. Their alleged fragile sensibilities (see the parody below) required men to refrain from certain behavior and language in their presence. In the past, chivalry was a given, (as one legendary story suggests) even to the point of gallantly doffing a cloak and throwing it over a mud puddle to protect the feet of a thusly perched woman—albeit a queen. Today it seems that some modern feminist women (e.g. MIT research biologist

Nancy Hopkins) want similar deference while paradoxically insisting that men treat women as equals in labor and most social circumstances. The brouhaha she created **cost Harvard president, Larry Summers, his job**. Vis a vis (Stereotypical findings show convincingly that stereotype threat significantly affects women's performance. These experiments strongly support the general assumption that it is the social stereotyping rather than any inherent biological traits, that accounts for the difference in male and female systemizing skills, and thus performance in mathematical exams or career choice. In light of all this evidence, one must doubt the assertions of Lawrence Summers and Simon Baron-Cohen that women are innately less capable of high-level mathematical achievement and are less represented at the extreme right-tail of the mathematical ability spectrum. Since the claims in question lend themselves well to further stereotyping, scientists and other public figures have a responsibility to ensure they are fully watertight before they are ever voiced. We cannot dismiss the achievement gap in math fields by simply writing it off as an immutable biological fact; rather, we should put our collective energy toward addressing the social factors that keep women from reaching their true potential.)

In a satirical retort one NY Times reporter dryly wrote: "The foul brute (Summers) may as well have rapped that women are "hos," or declared that they should be kept barefoot and pregnant. Nancy Hopkins' remarkable feminist exercise in self-parody, told reporters that she "felt I was going to be sick," that "my heart was pounding and my breath was shallow, and that she had to flee the room because otherwise "I would've either blacked out or thrown up." Such fatuous feminist fulminations may have been good fun in past eras, as have been the eviscerations of Hopkins as a latter-day "Victorian maiden exposed to male coarseness, [who] suffers the vapors and collapses on the drawing room carpet in a heap of crinolines." This may indeed be a case where a woman wants her 'cake and whatever...

CHAPTER 10

AWAKE

1. **GOOD OLD DAYS** In some ways this book may seem like an appeal to return to simpler, **bygone days**. (As if this were even a possibility.) This is not my intention. I would rather like to ask the reader certain questions, some of which may appeal to a particular view of history. So let's return to the **good old days** of caring when Americans were deeply religious, industrious, and had fundamental everyday morality! Right? But WAIT! Do you really want to go back to those "good old days?" A friend's recent Email helped me to conceptualize a more personal view of my own life in the good old days. I'm talking about the good old days from which some (fewer than today) of us survived the days and the daze of birth trauma, many times at home—mine was. In those days birthing took place without benefit of pelvic blocks or C sections. In those good old days pregnant mothers smoked cigarettes and drank cocktails. My mother gobbled aspirin, ate pickled pigs feet, and bleu cheese. She even ate uninspected tuna from a can. She wasn't obese and didn't have diabetes symptoms until she was 80 something. After my mother's uneventful four-hour labor, I was born, held upside down, swatted, cried, and put to bed on my tummy without fear of *crib death*. I went to sleep in a slatted baby crib covered with yellow lead-base paint.

    In those good old days I rode in cars with rumble seats without restraints or restrictions, no booster seats, no seat belts, no air bags. Riding in the back of an open pick-up with a bunch of other kids to Boy Scout meetings was ordinary transportation. I drank water from a garden hose or sometimes from an actual stream. I ate pancakes, cupcakes, ding-dongs, white bread, real butter, and greasy bacon. I made Kool-Aid with gobs of white refined sugar then tried to sell it for a nickel a glass at my street corner Kool-Aid stand. Actually, by the end of the day, my cousin and I drank most of it. After all this nutritional decadence I survived, probably because most of my free time was spent outside actively playing—no TV and no computer games to addict me and keep me indoors absorbing my waking hours. I tasted a few mud pies, poured salt on snails, and set off firecrackers with a 'punk' on the 4th of July. I was given a BB gun for my 11th birthday. I rode my bike several blocks to school, without a helmet. Even today, just the faint memory of those good old days, *makes me want to run with scissors!*

But ... such a big word ... BUT ... one person's junk is another's treasure. The good old days carried a whole bunch of junk.

2. Milton, Robert, 2005 **The True Believers**. Author house, Bloomington Indiana USA

3. Subjugation and even the **murder of women** is central in all of the desert religions. Islam—through the God/Allah invention—seems to be the very worst. The only way to get the superior sex of the species to subordinate them selves is by inventing "religious terminology" which has at its core a "male god".
Oh, by the way, on the subject of benign Muslim heritage in America—
Have you ever been to a Muslim hospital?
a Muslim orchestra?... a Muslim band march in a parade?
Have you witnessed a Muslim charity?
Have seen Muslims shaking hands with Muslim Girl Scouts?
Have you seen a Muslim Candy Striper in any hospital?
Or seen a Muslim do anything that contributes positively to the American way of life?
—Didn't think so ... In God /Allah We Trust!?? Just coexisist!

5. **Perhaps** Unbelievable to some—but the speech below from **Winston Churchill**, was delivered in1899 when he was a young soldier and journalist. It probably sets out the realistic view but expresses it in the wonderful Churchillian turn of phrase of which he was a master. Sir Winston Churchill was, without doubt, considered one of the greatest men of the late19th and 20th centuries. He was a brave young soldier, a brilliant journalist, an extraordinary politician and statesman, a war leader and British Prime Minister. He was a prophet in his

own time. He died on 24th January 1965, at the grand old age of 90. After a lifetime of service to his country, was accorded a State funeral.

HERE IS THE SPEECH:

"How dreadful are the curses which Mohammedanism lays on its votaries! Besides the fanatical frenzy, which is as dangerous in a man as hydrophobia in a dog, there is this fearful fatalistic apathy. The effects are apparent in many countries, improvident habits, slovenly systems of agriculture, sluggish methods of commerce, and insecurity of property exist wherever the followers of the Prophet rule or live.

A degraded sensualist deprives this life of its grace and refinement, the next of its dignity and sanctity. The fact that in Mohammedan law every woman must belong to some man as his absolute property, either as a child, a wife, or a concubine, must delay the final extinction of slavery until the faith of Islam has ceased to be a great power among men.

Individual Muslims may show splendid qualities, but the influence of the religion paralyses the social development of those who follow it. No stronger retrograde force exists in the world. Far from being moribund, Mohammedanism is a militant and proselytizing faith. It has already spread throughout Central Africa, raising fearless warriors at every step; and were it not that Christianity is sheltered in the strong arms of science, the science against which it had vainly struggled, the civilization of modern Europe might fall, as fell the civilization of ancient Rome ..."

Sir Winston Churchill; (Source: The River War, first edition, Vol II, pages 248-250 London).

Churchill saw it coming ... Subjugation of women is central in all of the desert religions.

6. Is **love synergistic**?

Through the use of Synergy humanity can effortlessly expand good, (i.e. through LOVE.) Synergy, while called by many names (including God, Spirit or 'the universe') is observable and verifiable naturalist empirical 'magic'. It is our earth's universal law, which exists in our abundant and constantly changing world. Through the power of Synergy, human beings have an invaluable tool for healing each other. Synergy dramatically promotes our ability to connect with "the other" and thereby positively add to the greater good. Synergy allows us to become consciously aware of our own changing brain structures as we interact.

Simply put, Synergy is "energy that expands through cooperation. In this way the whole becomes greater than the sum of the parts" A natural power is generated in cooperative endeavors, which far exceeds the capabilities of any individual acting alone. The birth of a child (the next generation) is an example.

7. **Chances are, you've heard the label of being a "right-brained" or "left-brained"** thinker. Logical—detail-oriented and analytical? That's left-brained behavior—Creative, thoughtful and subjective? Your brain's right side functions stronger or so long-held assumptions suggest.

But newly released research from University of Utah neuroscientists assert that there is no evidence within brain imaging that indicates some people are right-brained or left-brained.

For years in popular culture, the terms left-brained and right-brained have come to refer to personality types, with an assumption that some people use the right side of their brain more, while some use the left side more.

Following a two-year study, University of Utah researchers have debunked that myth through identifying specific networks in the left and right brain that process lateralized functions.

Original Research: Full open access research for "An Evaluation of the Left-Brain vs. Right-Brain Hypothesis with Resting State Functional Connectivity Magnetic Resonance Imaging" by Jared A. Nielsen, Brandon A. Zielinski, Michael A. Ferguson, Janet E. Lainhart, and Jeffrey S. Anderson in *PLOS*

ONE. Published online August 14 2013 doi:10.1371/journal.pone.0071275

8. **Oxytocin known also as the love hormone. Without it, we assume that love, as human beings know it, would never take place.** Oxytocin is a powerful neurotransmitter hormone. When we hug or kiss a loved one oxytocin levels drive up. It also acts as a neurotransmitter in the brain. In fact, the hormone plays a huge role in pair bonding. Prairie voles, one of nature's most monogamous species, produce oxytocin in spades. This hormone is also greatly stimulated during sex, birth, breast-feeding—the list goes on.

REFERENCES AND READINGS

Ann, Martha; Imel, Dorothy. 1993. *Goddesses in the World of Mythology.* New York: Oxford

Alter, Adam. 2013. *Drunk Tank Pink.* New York: Penguin Group

Austen, Halle. 1990. *The Heart of the Goddess.* Oakland, CA. Wingbow Press

Blyth, Myrna. 2004. *Spin Sisters: How the Women of the Media Sell Unhappiness and Liberalism to the Women of America.* New York: St. Martin's

Dawkins, Richard. *1998. Unweaving the Rainbow, Delusion and the Appetite for—Wonder.* Boston: Houghton Mifflin Co.

Dawkins, Richard. 2011. *The Magic of Reality.* New York: Free Press

Dennett, Daniel. 1995. *Darwin's Dangerous Idea: Evolution and the Meaning of Life.* New York: Touchstone

Gadon, Elinor. 1989. *The Once and Future Goddess.* San Francisco: Harper Collins

Harris, Judith. 2009. *The Nurture Assumption.* New York: Free Press

Harris, Sam. 2005. *The End of Faith.* New York: WW Norton and company.

Harris, Sam. 2012. *Free Will.* New York: Free Press

Milton, Robert. 2005. *The True Believers.* Bloomington Indiana: Author house

Mundy, Liza. 2012. *The Richer Sex.* New York: Simon and Schuster

Nanda, Meera, 2004. *Prophets facing Backwards.* New Brunswick: Rutgers Press

Pinker, Steven. 2002. *The Blank Slate.* New York: Penguin Books

Rosin, Hanna. 2012. *The End of Men.* New York: Penguin Group

Sandberg, Sheryl. 2013. *Lean In.* New York: Alfred a. Knopf

Stone, Merlin. 1976. *When God was a Woman.* New York: Harcourt Brace & Co.

Weinberg, Steve. 2001. *Facing up: Science and its Cultural Adversaries.* Cambridge, Mass: Harvard University Press

INDEX

t

A

Abraham 55
abuse ix
Adam 51
Adam and Eve 52
American democratic system 13
Amsterdam airport urinals 70
Arab Autumn 76
Arab Spring, 76
Armageddon 2
Art form xviii
ayurvedic medicine 40

B

backward decline 41
Beauvoir 44
belief 11
beliefs 24
Big Three religionists 93
billionaires 13
blue lights 72
Blyth 95
brain scans 45
brute strength 48, 52
Buddha xi
burka 24
bus-driver 8

C

candlelit baths 31
capitalism 13
Centenarian Study 16
Channing Tatum 57
child abuse 69, 70, 137
chosen people 61
Christian church fathers 61
Christian fundamentalists 9
Christianity 63
Clare Booth 30
Cognitive Dissonance 80
Coleridge 65
Communist Manifesto 12
Constantine 64
contemporary women 28
corticoid receptors 73
Creation science 39
cultural science 37

D

daily prayers 50
Darwins evolution 71
Dawkins x, 69, 70, 98, 136, 151
death x, 3, 98
death and resurrection 50
debt 14
denial 13
desert religions 23, 92
Desert religions 74
Dever 56
divorce rates 78
dragon 89
DREAMING 103
Drunk Tank Pink xi
Dualistic ideology 28

E

ecclesiastic authorities 7
Egypt 8, 49, 51, 53, 57, 58, 59, 60, 130, 140
Egyptian law of divorce 58
Einstein 5, 20, 37, 38
empirical evidence 90
Epic of Gilgamesh 54
Eve 7
evolving at a faster rate 43
Exodus 53, 56, 59, 62, 127, 130, 131

F

Facebook 93
faith oriented science 34
famine 17
fatal accidents 17
Father Knows Best 12
Father or Abba 77
Faustus story 103
Fifty Shades of Grey 31
financial crash of 1929 12
flood 54
for-profit schools 14
Founding Fathers 9
free-market 14
free will x
Freud 28, 65, 66, 141
fuzzy mental viewpoints 89

G

Gadon 56
Galileo 89
gender equality 50
George Washington 9
Girl with the Dragon Tattoo xviii
God or the Goddess 87
Godot xvii
gods and goddesses 86
Göering 20
Google 16
green flash xiii

H

Hard science 44
Harris x
Harry Harlow 68
Hawaii xiii
Hebrew traditions 75
Hindu religion 33
holding office 75
holy-book cosmologies 41
Homo sapiens ix, xii, 88
hope xvi
human brain 44
Hurricane Katrina 71
Hurricane Rita 71
hypnotism 71

I

I AM 77
iceberg 66
illuminated light bulb 72
Indias female economy 27
Internet and mobile device 91
intuitive gender 36
intuitive gifts of knowing 32
intuitive guess 6
Ishmael 55
Isis 49

J

Jehovahs chosen 55
Jesus 62
Joseph 57
Joseph Smith 90
Journal of Surgical Research 48
Judith Harris 67

K

killing fields 19
King Saud University 19
Krishna 34

L

laggard xviii
land of milk and honey 60
Las Vegas 89
Leprechauns xiii
Levitical priests 56

M

magic 34
Male/Female check box 45
male sovereigns 2
Mardi Gras charade 8
medical school 30
Meera Nanda 38
meme xii
Menehune xiv
Merneptah victory stele 60
metaphysics 35
Mohamed 90
Monticello 10
Mothers 23
multi-orgasmic 18
Mundy 88
Muslim 18
Muslim Quran 25
mysticism 38
mythology and magic 92

N

naturalism 97
New Age xiii, 4
New Age supporters 39
nomads 59
non-resolved war 21
numerology 34

O

Occams razor 35
Old Testament scriptural 52, 54
Oneness 76
Osiris 49

P

Palm Springs 30
passive and inferior being 52
patriarchal power 37
Pavlovlan-like animal 20
PC tolerance 98
pharmaceutical companies 15
physical strength 7, 11
picture of two eyes 72
poetry xv
postwar 50s 12
Potiphar 57
psychoanalysis 65
purdah 26

Q

quantum physics 36
Quran 61

R

rainbow 54
Rationalization and Denial 94
reincarnation 4
religious law? (1) 22
Reuters 18
Richard Rodriquez 74
rocket scientist 14
Rosie the riveter 12
Rosin 88

S

Sally Hemings 10
Sandberg 44, 46
Sarah 55
Saudi Arabia 19
savvy young people 92
Senate 1
Sharia law 19, 75, 117
skepticism 5
slave ix
slaves 2

155

Spin Sisters 95
spirituality 85
State legislators 66
stereotypes 96
stereotypical 45
Stockholm felons 80
Stockholm syndrome 79
St Paul 62
St. Paul 90
stress 73
superior gender 3
supernatural phenomena 33
surgeon 48
Susan B. Anthony 49
Synergism 87
synergistic miracle 96
synergized male companions 95

T

tent dwellers 60
terrycloth mom 68
testosterone 8, 29
The Big Three 2, 7, 24, 25, 32, 51, 52, 70, 74, 75, 77, 78, 93, 96, 97, 130
Thecla 63
The Flexxible Brain 91
The Hindu News 32
theological dictum 51
the other xvi, xviii, 3, 6, 7, 25, 31, 87, 88, 94, 95, 96, 98, 99, 100, 101, 102, 112, 120, 127, 135, 149
Thomas Jefferson 9
threshold for pain 17
Twitter 93

U

unconscious ix
unconscious conditioning 70
unconscious gender bias 66
unconscious influences xvi, 66, 68, 71, 72
unconscious mind is the rule 73
United States workforce 1

universal truth 40
U.S. Supreme court 15
Utnapashtim 54

V

Vedic 42

W

W. Dever 53
weaker sex 21
Winston Churchill, 99
women are considered footnotes 74
women cover 18
Women evolve hotter 43
Womens Liberation Movement 27

X

X chromosome 17

Y

Yahweh 50, 52, 55, 57, 58, 59, 78
Yahweh, 58

CPSIA information can be obtained at www.ICGtesting.com
Printed in the USA
LVOW11s1214221213

366256LV00001B/54/P